BOEING 777

AIRLIFE'S AIRLINERS 1

BOEING 777

Philip Birtles

Airlife
England

First published in the UK in 1998
by Airlife Publishing Ltd

British Library Cataloguing in Publication Data
A catalogue record for this book
is available from the British Library

ISBN 1 85310 945 2

Printed in Singapore

Airlife Publishing Ltd

101 Longden Road, Shrewsbury SY3 9EB, England

COVER: A6-EMD, the first of seven 777-21Hs delivered to Emirates. *Austin J. Brown*

PREVIOUS PAGE: The first Boeing 777 taxies onto the runway at Boeing Field ready
for departure on another test flight in the comprehensive flight development
programme involving up to nine aircraft with three different engine types. *Boeing*

BELOW: G-RAES showing off British Airways' new corporate image introduced in
mid-1997. *BA*

CONTENTS

INTRODUCTION

With the serious competitive market place largely generated by the products of Airbus Industrie in Europe, Boeing needed to have a major change of culture to survive. The company no longer had a captive market, and needed not only to reduce its costs and prices to the airlines, but also to change from producing an aircraft that Boeing thought the airlines would want, to designing and building an aircraft which fitted more closely the airlines' operational requirements. Boeing still has not gone all the way with customer as partner, but many lessons have been learned, and the next major project will take the previously very conservative organisation even further into producing the aircraft needed by the customer.

In producing the 777, Boeing had the customers, suppliers and sub-contractors as partners, the major risk partners being the engine manufacturers. It is becoming increasingly uneconomic for three major engine manufacturers to be supplying expensive newly developed engines for a new airframe, which may take years to gain enough sales volume to provide a reasonable return on investment. The engine manufacturers are being pushed into supplying even more reliable engines at keener competitive prices. This means that not only do the companies not earn sufficient on the initial sale, but the high reliability requirements — and the resultant penalties if these standards are not achieved — place the return on overall investment even further away. The move is now beginning to tend towards the demand for exclusive engine supply, as used to be the case in the past, joint venturing with competing manufacturers, or simply deciding that it is not worth the additional investment. This is a commercial hazard to the airlines, who may have selected an engine for early versions of an aircraft, and then find the competitive pressures force them to select a new supplier for later versions.

In the case of Rolls-Royce and Pratt & Whitney, the Trent and PW4000 turbofans were derivative engines from earlier

models, reducing development costs and technical risk, but perhaps also reducing the long-term potential of advanced development. However, the General Electric GE90 turbofan was developed as a new engine, based on an accumulation of past experience. This at least allowed a greater development potential, but costs were higher and technical risk greater, resulting in some unexpected problems, and consequent delays in service entry. So far, General Electric has sold fewer of its engines on the 777 than the other two engine manufacturers, making a return on its investment a long way off, something that brings a natural reluctance to invest in more powerful developments without a reasonable chance of profit.

In producing the 777, Boeing not only opened up its design offices to the customer and suppliers, but also a television team was allowed unprecedented access, as was a journalist called Karl Sabbagh, who wrote the companion book to the TV series.

Whenever Boeing brings out a new type of airliner, the ini-tial production batch contains little more than service-ready development aircraft. The first one of each new type is Boeing-owned, and is used entirely for development, never entering service with any airline. As with any complex aircraft, the design may never stop, and if one waited to achieve the engineers' ideal product, the building would never start. However, there has to be a point when design is frozen, and metal is cut. As a result, the early models of the 777 delivered to United, British Airways and Cathay Pacific, are not what was really required in terms of payload and range, but once the increased all-up weight versions become available, with additional fuel capacity and increased power, they will probably be allocated to

BELOW: Although the 777 is Boeing's largest twin-jet airliner, the clean and functional design reduces the overall bulk. The prototype development aircraft N7771 WA001 is seen flying above the clouds on one of the many test flights leading to certification. *Boeing*

ABOVE: The Boeing-owned first development 777 N7771 WA001 made its maiden flight from Paine Field on 12 June 1994, and visited London Gatwick on 12 September 1995. *Nick Granger*

ETOPS-rated routes, and the earlier versions will replace older aircraft on less demanding services. Improvements are continually being made to modern airliners, most of which can be retrofitted if the manufacturer is able to sell them to the airline, although any faults found during service are usually corrected by the manufacturer as part of the product support service.

As a marketing ploy, no doubt to combat the keenly competitive Airbus products, Boeing decided to offer ETOPS as part of its service-ready programme. There are a number of airlines who do not need ETOPS, either because the aircraft are being operated on short-range dense routes, such as in Japan, or the airline's route structure does not require long over-water flights. On top of this, although Boeing offers an ETOPS-capable aircraft, the purchasing airline must still satisfy its own national airworthiness authority that it is capable of operating to the ETOPS standard.

For Boeing to undertake this ETOPS-ready capability was not only challenging technically and operationally, but also it was a very costly addition to the development programme, and added a year to the flight development tasks. With all three engine manufacturers being encouraged to achieve ETOPS, a total of nine Boeing 777s had to be allocated to the flight testing programme, three of each engine type, of which at least one had

to be ETOPS-dedicated, and have to fly successfully for at least 1,000 hours without an ETOPS-related fault. An engine could operate almost the entire flight programme, and then have a fault which required going back to the start. Such a drastic move was avoided by using already mature engines, with the agreement of the certification authority. When engine developments are added, further ETOPS testing is required to ensure a safe and reliable operation.

Boeing will need to sell a considerable number of 777s, in competition with Airbus, to justify the cost and time of service-ready ETOPS. In many cases it probably would have been more cost effective to allow the experience to build up in service, as previously with the 757 and 767. On the positive side, the lessons learned will be used for future new airliner development, making ETOPS easier to obtain as part of the overall programme.

The Boeing 777 was planned, therefore, to be an advanced and very capable new aircraft, with the duty of carrying people and cargo worldwide at economical cost. It was also planned to be capable of continuous development over many years, particularly as the engine manufacturers continue to improve their products, to meet the continuing demands of Boeing and the airlines to fly more people further.

This book, the first of a new series, takes this most up-to-date and contemporary aircraft as its subject. After reading it, the author is sure that will show without doubt that the Boeing 777 is the 21st Century Jet.

ACKNOWLEDGEMENTS

The creation of a book is often a solitary activity in putting the words to paper or today entering words into the computer. It does, however, require a great deal of research which cannot be achieved without unselfish help from a large number of people who already have a busy agenda but kindly make time to provide the reference data from their files.

Without the help of those representing representing The Boeing Company — Kirsti Dunn in Seattle, Dick Kenny and Peter Middleton in the UK — there would have been no point in even starting the book. Additional help from my good 'Comet' friend Bob Hood of the Seattle Museum of Flight was much appreciated. Nearer to home David Hedges and Captain Kevin Mottram of British Airways provided me with enthusiastic first-hand access both for pictures and flight information. On the day of the visit to Kevin Mottram, I met by chance Nick Granger, who allowed me full access to his collection of TriStar photos for the second book in this series just when I thought I would never find enough pictures, and also checked the production list for this book.

Because a book of this nature requires a large number of colour photographs, and the reader expects to see more than just the manufacturer's stock material, I have had a great deal of support from the airlines and also from my good friend Johann Prozesky, based with Gulf Air in Bahrain who organised the night-time turnaround shots of the Cathay Pacific 777, and his son Martin who gained access to the airport and apron areas in Tokyo taking the excellent working shots of the 777s with ANA and JAL, as well as obtaining some JAS photos.

One of the problems with an aircraft in the early years of its commercial operation is that not many airlines have it in service yet, and therefore there is a challenge to obtain enough variation of visual material. However, with the help of the majority of the current airlines and Rolls-Royce, a broad selection has been obtained. Keely Podbury of Andy Plews Associates provided his entire office file on United Airlines, as did Daniel O'Connor of All Nippon Airways and Geoffrey Tudor of Japan Airlines. Ernest Alsina of Egyptair helped me to obtain photos of the proving flights to London and additional material was sent by A. H. Esmat from Cairo. Russell Stenhouse of Millennium Public Relations provided considerable information on Cathay Pacific, and Ameer Toor of Singapore Airlines sent details of the enthusiastic introduction of the 777. Fadhilah Mustaffa sent me the latest pictures following 777 delivery to Malaysian and a most comprehensive media pack was supplied by Emirates. Finally I thank my wife Martha, who provides complete support and encouragement while I am collecting data, photos and pounding the keyboard, as well as her relief that I have at last learned to use a PC. If I have missed anyone out, I sincerely apologise, and any errors in the book are entirely my own, unless I can find someone else to blame.

Philip Birtles
Stevenage, July 1997

1 EVOLUTION

The Boeing 777 jet airliner is a new aircraft from the famous United States West Coast aerospace company, covering the slot in the market perceived by Boeing between the high capacity long-range 747 Jumbo Jet, and the smaller twin-jet 767 family of regional airliners. The 777 was targeted as a replacement for ageing DC-10s and TriStars, providing an updated, economic airliner for long-haul but less dense intercontinental routes.

COMPETITION

In the post-World War II world Boeing built up a formidable reputation for its jet airliners throughout world airlines. Boeing's only major competition came initially from Douglas with its DC-8, of similar size to the Boeing 707, and DC-9, which competed directly with the Boeing 737. However, stronger competition was to come from Europe with the development of the Airbus family of airliners, produced by a consortium of aerospace manufacturers from Britain, France and Germany, with modest contributions from Spain and Holland. The Airbus family commenced with the twin-engined A300, which is still being produced as the larger capacity A300-600, and was followed by the shorter, longer-range A310. Airbus then entered the narrow-bodied jet airliner field with the A320, (later developed into the longer A321) and the shorter A319, the latter two assembled in Germany, while all the other Airbus planes have been assembled at Toulouse in France.

BELOW: The first Boeing commercial jet airliner was the 707 which entered transatlantic service with PanAm at the end of 1958, just beaten by the BOAC Comet 4s across the Atlantic. With advancing age and more stringent noise regulations, few 707s remain in regular service, although they are used as freighters, military tankers or for specialist operations. MEA was still operating OD-AGU, a 707-347C-H, in September 1995, when it visited Rhodes. *Philip Birtles*

Taking the standard wide-bodied fuselage of the A300 and A310, Airbus then developed the longer-range, higher-capacity A330 and similar A340 — the former with two engines, the latter four — to provide the airlines with flexibility of operation, while (like Boeing) giving commonalty of systems. Also like Boeing, Airbus Industrie has always aimed to use the latest technology in its aircraft and, wherever possible, the flight characteristics are similar to keep crew training to a minimum across all types. The A340, and in particular the A330, are probably the closest competitors to the 777, and gained a lead on it as the Airbus products were available sooner. Currently the only Boeing aircraft which does not have direct competition is the 747, and Airbus is planning to correct that omission with its next generation of long-range, high-capacity airliners.

BOEING

Boeing has been in the airline business since the 1930s, although the company was beaten to dominance of the market-place at the time by Douglas Aircraft with the DC-2 and, more spectacularly, improved DC-3 airliners. Indeed, so successful was the seeemingly ubiquitous DC-3 that the immediate post-war market was flooded with ex-military versions. The DC-3 was developed into the larger four-engined DC-4 during World War II, to be followed by the longer DC-6, and the ultimate DC-7. Meanwhile Lockheed developed the Constellation family of airliners during the late 1930s into the postwar era.

Boeing concentrated its talents on bombers during World War II, starting with the famous B-17 Flying Fortress and followed by the larger and longer-range B-29 Superfortress. As well as continuing with bomber designs into the jet age, Boeing had returned to the commercial airliner market by adapting the

B-29, with a new double-decker fuselage, into the Stratocruiser.

By combining its experience with jet bombers and piston-engined transports, and with the help of the USAF, the company was able to develop the Boeing 707 four-jet airliner from the military C-135 transport. Later the same basic airframe would be used in a number of roles, particularly as the KC-135 air-to-air refuelling tanker. The Boeing 707 entered service with PanAm in the latter part of 1958. From this initial design was progressively developed a family of jet airliners including the tri-jet 727; the best selling 737, the smallest member; and then the largest of all the Boeing 747, capable of carrying up to 400 passengers over long ranges. In fact the latest model of the 747 can fly from London to Sydney with a full load of passengers, stopping once at Singapore.

The Boeing family of jet airliners was further extended by the 757 (as a larger, longer-range 727 replacement) and the wide-bodied 767. The 707, 727, 737 and the 757 all used a common narrow-body fuselage cross-section for ease of production and to keep costs down; furthermore, many of the systems were similar, to give users of a number of members of the fleet a cost-effective answer in terms of spares and maintenance. Additionally, the Boeing 757 and 767 were designed with common cockpits, and comparable handling characteristics, in order to avoid costly crew training across the two types.

TOP: Following the long-range 707/720 four-jet airliner series, Boeing then produced the regional 727. It was similar in layout to the Hawker Siddeley Trident but the 727 was a much greater sales success with some 1,800 aircraft produced. Many remain in airline service — here, Air Algerie 727-2D3A 7T-VEH is seen on approach to Heathrow in June 1997. *Philip Birtles*

ABOVE: The world's best-selling airliner, and Boeing's smallest, is the 737. With sales approaching 3,000 aircraft, some of the earlier examples have now been retired because they have reached the end of their economic structural lives. However, the type is not only still in production, but continues in development in three new technology versions. One British low-cost 737 operator is easyJet, which uses its direct booking phone number as part of the colour scheme. This photograph shows easyJet 737-300 G-EZYD leaving the company's Luton base in July 1997. *Philip Birtles*

For the 777 Boeing started with a clean sheet of paper to allow completely fresh thinking on materials, systems, engineering, manufacture and even the layout flexibility of the cabin. What the company had was simply an objective: to transport people and cargo safely and cost-effectively over intercontinental routes. Nevertheless, despite this starting point, though the Boeing 777 certainly uses advanced technology in its construction and systems, it is very much an evolutionary aircraft. What is revolutionary is the process by which it was produced. A great deal of the technology has been proven and developed in earlier designs, such as the Electronic Flight Instrumentation System (EFIS) in the cockpit, which

was first used by Boeing on the flightdecks of the Boeing 757 and 767 family. These replaced the older analogue flight instrumentation — at first with small colour cathode ray tube screens, and later liquid-crystal displays, developed in turn from the latest Boeing 747-400. These displays give reliable and clear cockpit readings, without moving parts, and only show the flight crew the information they want when they want it. The entire system is driven by on-board computers, and the displays are bright enough to be clear in all light levels, without giving unwelcome glare. Fly-by-wire was also adopted by Boeing for the first time on the 777, replacing all the heavy, maintenance-intensive control cables and pulleys with lighter wiring, by which electrical signals are sent to servo motors, so that the controls are moved when the signal is received from the flight-deck from the traditional control column. Increased use of composite materials, not just in fairings but also load-bearing structure, reduces weight and maintenance time, as well as costs.

The start of the evolution of the Boeing 777 can be traced back to the latter part of 1986, when the company was trying to interest the world's airlines in a longer-range version of the Boeing 767. The general response was that they wanted something between the Boeing 747 and the 767 in terms of cabin size and range. It had taken only a short time in airline service

ABOVE: Apart from being nicknamed 'Jumbo Jet', the Boeing 747 has not been given a name: recently, however, its earlier versions have started to be called the 747 Classic. The four-engined 747 is the largest airliner from Boeing and has also the honour of being the world's largest commercial airliner, although this is now being challenged by the Airbus. Around 700 of the earlier 747-100, and -200 and -300 series were built, many remaining in current service. Northwest 747-251B N615US, the 165th 747 off the Everett production line, is ready for departure from Gatwick in August 1995. *Philip Birtles*

RIGHT: The major development of the Boeing 747 is the -400, which has the extended upper deck of the -300, improved wing aerodynamics, developed fan engines and greater fuel capacity giving improved economy and longer range. The aircraft also uses the glass cockpit technology developed for the Boeing 757/767 aircraft, and is normally operated by two crew. Japan Airlines 747-446 JA8902 shows the winglets, generous flaps and three-leg main undercarriage during final approach to Heathrow in June 1997. *Philip Birtles*

for Boeing to discover that when the 767's cabin size was right, its range capability was too short and, additionally, its wing was not large enough to take the aircraft up to an efficient cruising altitude. With a redesigned wing, the aircraft could fly nearly 7,000 miles (11,263km), but with that range airlines required more passenger density — more seats — which needed a longer fuselage length. Double-deck designs were considered, with a raised humped-back rear cabin, but these increased drag unacceptably.

Finally, in October 1988, after looking at a variety of 767 variations none of which satisfied the market, the design team

made the logical decision to investigate a totally new design since the cost savings of a derivative were being lost. The initial data for the 777 was targeted to be ready before Christmas 1988.

However, it was the revolutionary Boeing concept of 'Customer as Partner' that was unique in producing the Boeing 777. This approach included not only Boeing's prospective external customer airlines, but also the internal customer, major groups working as design/build teams (DBT) to overcome together the challenges of producing this new airliner on time, and within budget, to the high quality required. In addition to this, one of the major challenges was to deliver to the airlines an ETOPS (Extended-range, Twin-engined Operations) capable aircraft right from the start, to allow full flexibility of operations in the unlikely event of an engine failure up to 180 minutes from the nearest suitable airfield. This requirement was a responsibility shared between Boeing and the three engine suppliers: Pratt & Whitney, General Electric and Rolls-Royce. In the past, ETOPS rating had only been achieved through experience gained by regular operations, proving the reliability of the engines and systems in service. This challenge would require working closely with the airworthiness authorities, additional reliability flight-testing, and during this development flying, no major faults being found that would question the integrity of the aircraft or engines.

The 'Customer as Partner' programme started with Boeing inviting teams from eight major airlines, covering the requirements not only of the North American market, but also Europe and Asia. The airlines involved in the definition of the 777 were United, American and Delta from the USA; British Airways from Europe; and Qantas, Cathay Pacific, Japan Airlines and All Nippon Airways representing the Pacific region. In the past, Boeing had been a very conservative organisation, making the concept of working together with the airlines something

that did not come naturally. The company had previously designed aircraft for perceived airline requirements, and then marketed them successfully, but Boeing felt that in the 'Customer as Partner' concept there was a more effective way to bring an even better product to the customer and, therefore, to be even more competitive as a company. In general, airlines rarely question the design technology of a new aircraft, unless it affects access, maintenance or reliability. The airlines' first priority is to satisfy their customers — the passengers — and their operational experience, something that aircraft manufacturers do not possess, is important in ensuring the best possible cabin layout. Boeing, therefore, allowed a large choice of positions for the galley and toilet locations, giving room and flexibility for a wide variety of seating configurations, in whatever class was required. Overhead luggage bins were designed to give maximum capacity, with ease of loading, without the hazards of dropping heavy items on fellow passengers. American Airlines was particularly concerned with the increased wingspan of the 777 not being compatible with the company's existing gates at the airports — so Boeing offered folding wingtips as an option. In fact, American was the only operator to require this capability, and since it has yet to place a firm order, this feature has not been adopted by any other airline, largely due to unnecessary complication and added weight.

There was a time when each new airliner had its power-plants specified by the airframe manufacturer, and the combination was certificated accordingly. Today's highly competitive market requires more customer freedom than this — and so today, after the aircraft has been selected, there follows the sales battle for the engines. Supplying the choice of more than one engine type increases the aircraft manufacturer's costs because

of additional design, manufacturing and certification. This they have been unwilling to shoulder on their own, and engine manufacturers have had to take much of the risk. However, with such keen competition, the engine manufacturers often have to reduce their prices to below an economical level to achieve the initial sale, in the hope that they will recover their investment over the years of service, by supplying spares and overhauls. This used to be a lucrative business in the past, but not only are modern fan-jet engines more reliable, the airlines are also insisting on extended warranties and guarantees, thus squeezing the engine manufacturers at both ends. Indeed, the cost of developing engines is now so great, with such an uncertain return on investment, that the wheel has turned full circle. Without the right engines, aircraft manufacturers cannot enter the right market, so — as is currently proposed for Airbus's new large airliner — the aircraft manufacturers are returning to the concept of the exclusive engine contract.

In the case of the Boeing 777, however, all three major international manufacturers offered engines for the aircraft: Pratt & Whitney specified derivatives of the PW4000 series which developed a thrust of 73,500lb (327kN) — a figure anticipated to grow to at least 84,600lb (377kN) in later versions. The other major American jet engine manufacturer, General Electric, offered the GE90 series developing initially 74,000lb (329kN), with growth at least to 84,700lb (377kN). Rolls-Royce offered the Trent starting at 71,200lb (318kN) thrust, and growing to 84,700lb (377kN) and beyond. However, thrust was not necessarily the most important measure, especially as all were very close — fuel consumption, purchase price, life cycle costs and any other inducements would help the airline to make the decision of which engine to use in its airframe.

ABOVE LEFT: The regional 757 was produced at the same time as the higher density 767 with an identical flightdeck, and similar handling characteristics to reduce crew conversion costs. Produced at Renton, and using the same fuselage cross-section as the 707, 727 and 737, the 757 continues in production, with development of the stretched -400 under way following a launch order from Delta. Here, Iceland Air 757-208 TF-FIH awaits departure from Heathrow in April 1997. *Philip Birtles*

ABOVE: The big brother of the 757 is the wide-bodied 767 produced at the Boeing Everett factory with the 747 and 777. It is currently built in two basic versions, the short -200 and the stretched -300, both of which can have extended-range capability. SAS 767-383ER SE-DKZ is seen on finals to Heathrow in June 1997 showing the flaps and forward trailing main undercarriage units. *Philip Birtles*

BELOW: United Airlines 777s are now becoming familiar visitors to Heathrow as the fleet grows in popularity. Here, United 777-222 N769UA c/n 26921, number 12 off the production line, which made its first flight from Everett on 13 June 1995 and was delivered on 28 June. It is seen ready for departure from Heathrow in November 1996. *Philip Birtles*

2 DESIGN

PLANS AND PARAMETERS

The Boeing 777 has become the biggest twin-engined jet airliner in the world, so it is unsurprising that the early planning processes focused on size, seating and flexibility. Studies included looking at the possibilities of two, three or four engines, but a twin-engined aircraft came out as the best all-round option giving lower fuel consumption and maintenance costs, despite the fact that a totally new engine would be required.

Ideally Boeing wished for a wingspan of around 60m (197ft); this size gained aerodynamic benefits, but avoided the need for upturned winglets at the wingtips, and still maintained an uncomplicated structure. This span, however, could cause problems with compatibility for existing airport boarding gates optimised for the McDonnell Douglas MD-11. As mentioned earlier, at the request of American Airlines, therefore, the option of a folding wingtip was offered. The new wing was designed aerodynamically for a speed of Mach 0.83: drag rise for advanced airfoils grows dramatically with increase in speed. The major advantages of the advanced wing designs now being developed are that the thicker section provides more space for fuel — increasing the range — and the lighter, stronger, structure gives improved payload.

Although Boeing started looking at the new generation of large-capacity long-range airliners later than their competitors — Airbus and McDonnell Douglas — the delay did confer two advantages: first, Boeing was able to go immediately for a larger aircraft with more range, a newer fuselage cross-section, a new interior and greater flexibility of operation. Second, the airline industry was in economic depression when the earlier types were launched, and so not many of them were sold and the 777 soon began to catch up.

The planning of the 777 saw many innovations perhaps best summed up by the words which were inscribed on the first aircraft below the flightdeck windows: 'working together'. The prospective airline customers and Boeing worked together to agree levels of quality and performance covering every aspect of the aircraft — such as drag, weight, reliability and load capacity. The challenging goals established by Boeing and the airlines for the 777 required Boeing to change, and as working together gathered momentum, the tremendous power of the approach was realised.

The first meeting of the 'working together' airlines was held at Boeing in January 1990, when each was given a questionnaire on what the 777 should be like. Two months later the answers had helped define the basic 'A-market' configuration of the new airliner, and the foundations for the later family of variants. A new corporate culture was generated by this exercise, and when United placed the launch order in October 1990 for up to 68 aircraft, a handwritten pledge for working together was signed by the airline and the manufacturer. This pledge, headed *B.777 Objectives*, stated that:

'In order to launch on-time a truly great airplane we have a responsibility to work together to design, produce and introduce an airplane that exceeds the expectations of flight crews, cabin crews, and maintenance and support teams and ultimately our passengers and shippers.

From day one:
Best despatch reliability in the industry.
Greatest customer appeal in the industry.
User friendly and everything works.'

The 777 design was, therefore, completely market-driven, with much of the specification being written by the airlines and then jointly developed. In previous programmes operators had rarely, if ever, been consulted, and the initial difficulties with the introduction of the Boeing 747-400, even though it was only a derivative, were not events which either the manufacturer or the airlines wanted to repeat.

As part of the new quality initiative, the 777 was to be what is known as 'service ready', with a despatch reliability of over 98 percent from delivery — instead of achieving these levels three or four years after entry into service. As part of this service-ready requirement, extended-range twin-jet operations (ETOPS) was essential to take advantage of the growing capability of the 777. 'ETOPS out of the box' was necessary for Boeing to compete effectively with the Airbus A330 large twin-jet, which had already entered service and was rapidly building up its ETOPS capability. In addition, there was also competition from the four-engined Airbus A340 and the tri-jet McDonnell Douglas MD-11, both of which could operate without restriction. Boeing, therefore, had to work closely with the airlines and the regulatory authorities to plan an acceptable method of evaluating the aircraft and engine combinations, to achieve this aspect of service ready on delivery of the initial aircraft.

In making it happen, Boeing had to alter the whole way of doing business, dumping old prejudices, and accepting previously alien concepts. The 'working together' programme inevitably exposed the company to greater confidentiality risks across a wider audience. The initial

ABOVE: The Boeing 777 was designed with a large enough wing to cope with all projected developments without expensive redesign. The outer sections were designed to have the provision for folding, to match existing DC-10 airport gates, but no airlines have taken up this option to date. *Boeing*

'working together' teams were formed with advisory full-time staff from four of the launch airlines, these being United, British Airways, All Nippon and Japan Airlines. This commitment by the airlines allowed continual advice to be given on reliability, maintenance and the technical manuals and, when appropriate, to deal with critical design issues. It was natural to work together to ensure that not only was the aircraft ready on time, but that the support was in place, and the airlines were themselves ready to put the aircraft into service. The working together was by no means one-sided: it was an essential team effort to ensure that all the demanding goals were met on time. A natural extension of this philosophy, was to instigate design build teams (DBTs), consisting of Boeing personnel across the responsibilities of the systems or structures being created, and often joined by the suppliers of the equipment, any sub-contractors and sometimes customer representatives. Gone were the days when a draughtsman produced a drawing, and 'threw it over the wall' for the factory to produce. Instead the design engineers worked closely with the production teams to ensure that what was being designed, could be produced on time, on cost, at the right weight, and with-

out last minute changes. Any problems were shared, avoiding conflict, and the combined talents of the team were responsible for the solution. This endeavour was complicated further by the geographical location of some of the manufacturers of major components of the aircraft: for example the composite rudder was produced in Australia, while the passenger entry doors were assembled in Japan.

A major innovation in the engineering of the 777 was the use of advanced computers, which could be programmed in the design process to check the three-dimensional fit of the various components, to ensure that there was no conflict or interference. The aim was for a 'paperless' design wherever possible, using a Boeing adapted Dassault/IBM CATIA computer-aided design system, the object being to reduce re-working and assembly error interferences — normally experienced in the early stages of a new aircraft — by 50 percent. This advanced technique reduced the use of the expensive full-scale design and engineering mock-ups, which had been

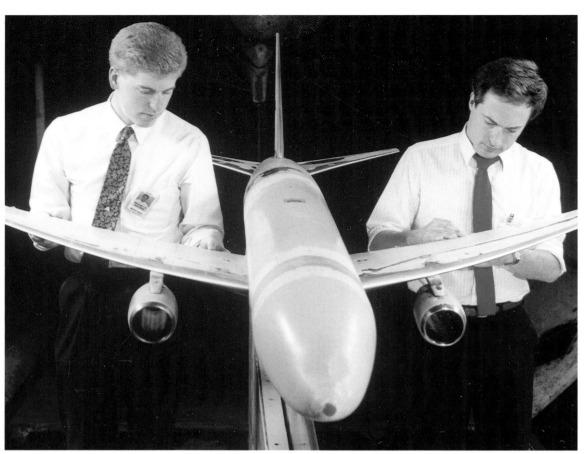

LEFT: Despite the sophisticated and powerful computers used to design the Boeing 777, it was still necessary to test the aircraft configurations in the wind tunnel. This helped validate and refine the computer models and provided valuable improvements to the design concept. *Boeing*

BELOW: Before the maiden flight of the first 777, Boeing test pilots flew 'Airplane Zero' in the Integrated Aircraft Systems Laboratory, allowing full checking of all the systems hardware and software prior to flight test of the actual aircraft. In control is Boeing Chief Test Pilot, John Cashman. *Boeing*

used in the past to check the fit of all the systems and components throughout the structure of the aircraft. They were really hand-made unflyable prototypes, which were built from wood and metal, becoming more complex as the design progressed. The information entered into the computers for the design could also be adapted for use in computer-aided manufacture, ensuring accurate high quality components, and a dramatic reduction in drawings and other paperwork. It also allowed the introduction of new computer-based assembly and installation factory control systems. Although setting-up costs were high, and the system is complex to operate, the better first time fit of parts on assembly more than paid for the initial costs of the system. CATIA is being further developed in the light of experience for later developments of the 777.

As a further part of the service-ready requirements, Boeing invested $370 million in an Integrated Aircraft Systems Laboratory (IASL) to replace the old 'Iron Bird' concept for testing the reliability of anything from individual components, to the integration of whole systems. By testing the operation of everything on the ground first, many potential faults could be identified in advance of full production commitment and flight test, reducing expensive re-work and costly delays. Boeing did not take anything for granted, but tested first to ensure the systems operated as required.

ABOVE: The new powerful **CATIA** computer-aided design system was used for the first time on the 777, and not only allowed the three-dimensional fit of components to avoid interference, but also helped to determine accessibility for maintenance. *Boeing*

BELOW: The Boeing 777 was the first jet airliner to be designed entirely using three-dimensional computer-aided design. This reduced the need for expensive engineering mock-ups, and ensured that the majority of parts fitted first time without expensive and time consuming redesign and rework. *Boeing*

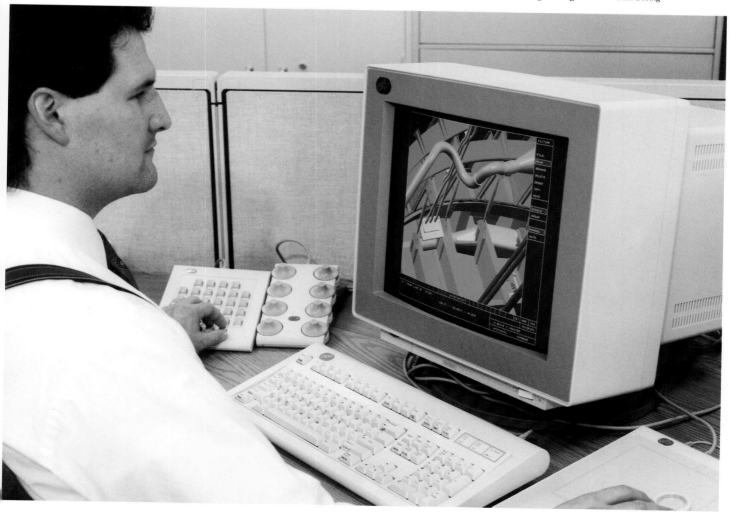

FLIGHT TESTING AND ETOPS

One of the most challenging targets that Boeing set for itself was to deliver a service-ready airliner, complete with ETOPS. In the past this had only been achieved after a number of years in normal commercial service, when the airliner had proved the reliability of the engines, airframe, equipment and the operation of the aircraft by the airline itself. ETOPS approval allows a twin-engined airliner to operate up to 180 minutes' flying time on a single engine from a suitable diversionary airfield, in the unlikely event of an engine failure. Not only is engine reliability and performance essential to achieving this approval, but the APU and certain key equipment must prove a high level of reliability and integrity, since they will be working under a greater load in an emergency diversion.

In May 1993 the FAA published the list of over 60 conditions for the Boeing 777 to achieve ETOPS on service entry. One of the key requirements was that one 777 powered by each of the three engine types must complete at least 1,000 cycles, simulating about three years of actual airline operation, and one of the engines installed on the test aircraft, complete with its pylon and systems, must have been through a 2,000 to 3,000-cycle ground test beforehand, and fly for a minimum of 500 cycles on the test programme. Any faults or failures encountered needed to be analysed to determine their effect upon the safety of ETOPS operations, the existing ETOPS-cleared airliners being taken as the benchmark.

Although modern engine development is becoming very sophisticated, it was still decided to test each of the manufacturers' engines on a flying test-bed, to validate the results achieved in the ground-based test cells. If the performance in both ground and flight testing was as predicted, it may be possible in the future not to flight-test engines before installation on the intended airframe.

ABOVE: In charge of the maiden flight of the first Boeing 777 was John Cashman, (left) the 777 chief pilot, and serving as first officer was Ken Higgins, Boeing Commercial Aeroplane Group Flight Test Director. Both are seen standing in front of the first aircraft — *Working Together*. *Boeing*

LEFT: The first prototype Boeing 777 on the runway at Everett ready for departure on its maiden flight on 12 June 1994. The full flight development programme was centred at the Boeing Flight Test Center at Boeing Field close to Seattle. *Boeing*

To achieve initial flight-testing of the Pratt & Whitney PW4084 engine, Boeing leased back the original 747 prototype from the Seattle Museum of Flight, and fitted the test engine to the No 2 position for flight-testing starting in June 1993. A year later, the aircraft was fitted with the Rolls-Royce Trent 884 engine, while the GE90 engine was flight-tested on another leased 747-100 from Mojave, California. During early test-cell running of the PW4084 engines, a thrust of 90,000lb (400kN) was reached, and although it had potential for greater power, testing was aimed at 88,200lb (392kN) thrust to allow an initial certification at 84,150lb (374kN). The Trent 800 series for the 777 used the well-tried three-shaft layout, developed in the earlier RB211 engine for the TriStar, but by fitting a larger fan, the potential thrust could reach 97,200lb (423kN) to power the larger 777s. Additional challenges had to be met by the engine manufacturers, as Boeing began offering higher weight versions of the 777 in the effort to carry a greater payload further than the competing Airbus airliners. One of the tests which the engines have to pass is to ensure that, should there be a fan-blade failure when the engine is running at full speed, it will be contained within the engine and not cause damage to any other systems or structure. This test was successfully passed by Pratt & Whitney in March 1993.

Meanwhile, the initial runs of the all-new GE90 engine in the test cell reached 105,400lb (469kN) thrust in April 1993, although the certification level was 87,300lb

(388kN), and the engine entered service with BA at a derated level of 78,750lb (350kN).

The ETOPS requirements needed additional design attention to the systems and equipment which had traditionally caused engine shut downs in the past. Not just the engine core, but also special design features were incorporated in the fuel, oil and control systems, examples of previous failures being caused by false high oil temperature readings. From 767 experience it was found that in an eight-year period only 30 percent of in-flight shutdowns (IFSD) had been caused by engine problems. Hydraulics and pneumatics caused 15 percent of the faults, electrical and APU snags caused 14 percent, and pressurisation, communications/navigation, autopilot, fire detection and a number of other faults accounted for the remainder of the IFDSs. All the systems' reliability was therefore evaluated to avoid unscheduled diversions, and to ensure there was sufficient redundancy available. During the flight-testing of the airframe/engine combinations, the higher thrust levels were used, and the engines were purposely run unbalanced to give the worst case. Alongside the engine which had already been ground-tested for up to 2,000 hours, was a brand new engine off the production line.

Nine 777s were allocated to the flight development programme — three more than would normally be used. Three 777s were allocated to standard certification flying, with two each allocated to each engine development programme. One of each of the engine types was used for normal engine certification purposes, while the others were used for the 1,000-cycle validation programme (CVP) which covered 1,800 flying hours.

Each CVP aircraft was used to validate the airframe/engine combination with emphasis on the ETOPS design features, secondary power generation, including the APU and general systems' integrity. The CVP was also used to validate the operations and maintenance training techniques, as well as the manuals. During the CVP about 85 percent of the flight cycles were completed in a time of less than 50 minutes, while the remainder varied from two to nine hours. Cruise altitudes varied from 18,000ft to 43,000ft (5,500-13,100m), with 65 percent at or above 35,000ft (10,700m). The temperatures experienced were from -20° to more than 100°F (-29° to +38°C). The APU made 1,900 starts, including 175 at altitude, and eight cycles were flown with one engine shut down, including a simulated three-hour emergency diversion. The final 90 flights were planned to be undertaken by each of the first airlines which would be using the ETOPS capability with each engine combination.

Both the FAA and the JAA were involved closely in defining the demanding standards which needed to be achieved, the FAA working towards 180-minute ETOPS,

RIGHT: Much of the cabin of the first 777 was filled with recording, telemetry and data equipment to allow both rapid analysis of results in real time, and also moving on to the next test rapidly. *Boeing*

BELOW: Not only was the cabin equipped with flight testing recording equipment, but tanks were installed for water ballast, to simulate varying loads, and to allow adjustment to the centre of gravity. *Boeing*

BELOW LEFT: Although only two pilots were aboard the Boeing 777 for its maiden flight, some 50 engineers were providing support from the ground, monitoring the handling qualities of the aircraft as well as the aircraft avionics, computer software and flight control systems through telemetry links via satellite. This centre was used for the early stages of the flight development programme, but once some maturity had been achieved, the flight-test data was monitored from on-board computer work-stations. *Boeing*

while the JAA considered 120-minute ETOPS more prudent. To obtain a JAA approval for 180 minutes, Boeing had to demonstrate at least 20,000 satisfactory in-service engine hours without a major failure for both the derivative Pratt & Whitney and Rolls-Royce engines, while the all-new GE engine would need to demonstrate 50,000 engine hours.

The Rolls-Royce Trent 884 powerplant for the 777 ran for the first time at Derby on 8 October 1993, achieving thrust well in excess of the 84,000lb (375kN) certification levels within two hours of the start of testing. The target for certification was February 1995, the first application being with Thai Airways in early 1996.

The first of the engines for the 777 to become airborne was the PW4084 fitted to the 747 test-bed on 10 November 1993, followed by the GE90 on its 747-100 test-bed on 6 December. During the first test, the GE engine ran for 3hr 40min and reached an altitude of 41,900ft (12,800m). This started the first phase of testing covering 30 sorties and 130 flight hours.

By early 1994, testing with the Trent 800 had been progressing so well that the decision was made to certificate at an initial thrust of 90,000lb (400.5kN) on the 777s for Thai Airways, instead of the previously planned 83,820lb (373kN). On bench tests the previous autumn, the Trent 800 had been achieving 93,000lb (414kN) of thrust, making the engine capable of meeting the potential demands of the higher gross weight versions of the 777. The GE90 and PW4084 engines were expected to be certificated at thrusts of 84,825lb (377kN) and 86,846lb (374kN) respectively. The GE90 engine experienced a setback when a fourth stage low-pressure compressor blade failed in a flight test. However, despite damaging other blades in the same stage, the problem was successfully contained within the engine. Despite this failure, the engine had been performing well, meeting all the operational goals and specifications, and General Electric was planning the increased thrust version for the growth versions of the 777, taking the engine up to 92,000lb (410kN) thrust with 99 percent commonalty with the initial engine.

The first of the three engines to receive FAA approval was the PW4084 in May 1994. Since the development of the engine had commenced, 23 test and development engines had been run for almost 2,500 hours in 6,000 cycles, 76 hours of which had been on the 747 test-bed. Although the engine was initially certificated at 84,600lb (375kN) thrust, it had been run at over 100,392lb (445kN) on test, giving an adequate margin.

ABOVE LEFT: The Boeing 777 prototype was able to demonstrate a good climb gradient after take-off, even after the simulated failure of one engine. *Boeing*

LEFT: The first Boeing 777 taxies onto the runway at Boeing Field ready for departure on another test flight in the comprehensive flight development programme. *Boeing*

By mid-1994 the FAA had set out its ETOPS requirements, after discussions with all parties, and had been joined by JAA at meetings of the Reliability Assessment Board. Key requirements included assessment of the Boeing design for reliability, in which ETOPS factors must be demonstrated in the aircraft design. Designs learnt from engine failures in other aircraft, such as the 767, were to be implemented, and flight-test requirements were to include a 3,000-cycle engine test, and a 1,000-airline operation cycle test before service entry, if ETOPS approval was to be awarded. Any faults experienced during flight-testing were to be evaluated, to ensure they were typical of normal airline operation, and a problem tracking programme was set up to ensure ETOPS- related issues were corrected before approval was given.

The start of an era began on 12 June 1994, when the first Boeing 777 made its maiden flight of 3hr 48min from Everett's Paine Field with chief test pilot John Cashman in command, assisted by Ken Higgins, director of flight test. The major part of the initial test was to check the operation of the fly-by-wire system, which was found to be very similar to the simulator. Bad weather kept the aircraft between 15,000ft and 18,000ft (4,600-5,500m) for most of the flight and, rather unusually for a first flight, one engine was shut down, allowed to cool, and restarted with a windmill relight. Snags experienced during this flight were minor and the aircraft had a scheduled four days' inspection before continuing the flight-test programme, soon moving operations to Boeing Field, near downtown Seattle. The second PW4084-powered 777 — destined for United — made its maiden flight on 15 July, by which time the company-owned first aircraft had flown 81 hours in 21 flights. Two more PW4084-powered 777s joined the basic certification programme, with a fifth aircraft to follow on ETOPS-dedicated operations. The flight-testing of this aircraft included eight 180-minute single-engine diversions, totalling 24 flying hours — the same as that experienced with the 767 during its first five years of airline service. The 90 cycles over 430 flying hours operated by United included simulated routes to Honolulu, Los Angeles and Washington.

Meanwhile, in July 1994 Pratt & Whitney revealed details of the growth PW4090 engine for the IGW versions of the 777, and that proposed to Korean as the powerplant for its aircraft. Although based on the existing PW4084 engine, the more powerful variant featured revised materials, revised high-pressure blade aerodynamics and further cooling on the high and low-pressure turbines, taking service thrust levels to more than 90,000lb (400kN). General Electric also outlined development plans for the uprated GE90 for the IGW variants of the 777. Starting with an initial 84,719lb (377kN) thrust engine, GE launched the 92,135lb (410kN) thrust version for certification in May 1996, with stepped improvements through 95,056lb (423kN) to 104,944lb (467kN), and ultimately to 115,000lb (510kN), to cover the requirements of the longer-range, heavier weight and stretched

versions of the aircraft. It was expected to keep the structure of the engine fairly standard up to 100,000lb (445kN) thrust, but after that the fan would need some redesign, including an increased diameter for the top end of the thrust range.

Although Rolls-Royce had hoped not to have to flight-test its engine before installation on the first 777 for Thai Airways, unexpected problems found with both the P&W and GE engines during their flight-testing required the Trent 800 to undertake the expensive flying test-bed programme. GE in particular had difficulties in meeting the certification schedule, initially because of unexpected low pressure turbine failures on the ground-test cells, caused by insufficient clearances.

The third aircraft joined the 777 test programme when it made its first flight on 2 August 1994. Meanwhile, testing on the first aircraft had progressed well, with only minor adjustments required. In early August the first aircraft completed successfully the demanding auto-braking and anti-skid system tests at Edwards Air Force Base in California. By this time the first three aircraft had flown more than 200 hours in around 70 sorties.

The P&W approach to ETOPS approval was to use a derivative engine, with smarter design, learning from past experience. As with all the engines, the PW4084 went through an extremely rigorous test phase, and there was a much greater degree of working with the customer before delivery of the first aircraft/engine combination. Particular emphasis was put on testing for excessive vibration, and development engines were run for over 2,500 hours and 6,000 flight cycles before certification. The engine also met its performance guarantees within better than one percent.

During the flight-testing of the early 777s, it was found that the drag was better than expected, allowing an increase from the planned Mach 0.83 cruise to over Mach

ABOVE: The demanding maximum energy rejected take-off test. The aim is to demonstrate that the brakes will stop the fully loaded aircraft following an aborted take-off. Using the Edwards runway, the 777 was accelerated to a take-off speed of more than 200mph (322km/hr), before the departure was abandoned. With the brakes glowing red hot, the aircraft was taxied-off the runway, and stopped for five minutes, to ensure no fire was started. In the test the brakes reached a temperature of 3,000°F (1,650°C) and the tyres deflated, but no permanent damage resulted. *Boeing*

ABOVE RIGHT: In mid-September 1994, the first Boeing 777 aircraft spent two weeks at Edwards AFB, using the vast airfield to undertake a rigorous series of pre-certification tests. Among these tests was velocity minimum unstick, which determines the minimum take-off speed, ensuring the aircraft does not stall during the ground run. The rear fuselage is protected from damage by an oak skid under the tail as the aircraft lifts off at minimum take-off speed. *Boeing*

BELOW RIGHT: While the flight-testing programme was under way, structural testing was continuing on the ground. In January 1995 the wings of the static test airframe were pulled up a distance of about 24ft (7m) above their normal position during the full scale destruct test. Computer-controlled hydraulic actuators applied loads of about 500,000lb (227,000kg) to each wing — the equivalent weight of a fully loaded 777 — and both wings broke at the predicted location. The test confirmed that the wings exceeded their maximum design requirements, which is 1.5 times the loads experienced in the most extreme flight conditions. The resulting test data allowed the Boeing engineers to determine the wing's extra development capability, and growth potential for future versions of the 777. In parallel with the static tests, a further structural airframe was being used for fatigue tests to simulate flight loads well in excess of anticipated levels. *Boeing*

0.84, which would reduce the flight time of an average long-range sector by about 40 minutes. The weight of the production standard aircraft was also on target. Adjustments were still being made to the aerodynamics, particularly to cure some tail buffet, and a large under-wing access panel had detached in-flight on at least three occasions. Excessive air conditioning noise had to be cured, and there was vibration of the nose-wheel doors, which was cured by fixing a baffle to divert the airflow. By early September 1994, the three test aircraft had flown more than 360 hours in over 110 sorties. The first 777 undertook minimum unstick trials at Edwards AFB during October, to determine the lowest speed for a given

weight at which the aircraft could take-off. The aircraft tail, protected by a laminated oak skid, was purposely dragged along the ground, to ensure the aircraft would not stall before take-off. This was a test devised following experience in the 1950s with the de Havilland Comet: if the Comet's nose was raised too high, it failed to get airborne. The reason had not been appreciated before, as earlier airliners had airflow driven over the wing surfaces by the propellers, a feature which was absent with jets.

By early October the three 777s in the test programme had flown more than 700 hours in over 200 flights. At the beginning of November the first aircraft made the maximum energy rejected take-off test, also at Edwards AFB, when — as was expected — the high kinetic heating blew out the tyres, but no fire was caused. The take-off weight was representative of the B-market/IGW version at 130,455lb (287,000kg). This test was the culmination of the demanding FAA certification tests which involved 57 flight hours and 163 landings at Edwards and Roswell New Mexico. Testing following this was to concentrate on ETOPS approval.

During engine runs on the Florida-based test-cell in September 1994, the No 8 production PW4084 suffered a failure as it was approaching the 700th cycle in a 3,000-cycle ground test programme. Out of a total of 70 around the engine, two variable vane-actuator arms failed but they were not expected to delay the certification date of the engine. It was possible that the failure was caused by vibration of the test engine, which was intentionally unbalanced as part of the endurance programme, but corrections were made in time for testing to restart by the end of October.

The GE90 suffered a high-pressure turbine-blade failure on 14 November 1994, which was traced to a casting defect, and it was not expected to delay the certification programme. The engine had already passed the crucial blade-off test, when one of the composite fan blades was severed at the root, and contained within the engine, although considerable damage resulted.

The achievement of ETOPS with the PW4084 engine was still challenging Boeing in the latter part of 1994, with the 1,000-cycle flight-testing planned to commence in November. The aircraft allocated to this programme, WA004, was in preparation, while the remainder of the flight-test programme was a little behind schedule, due to the adjustments being made as a result of faults found during testing. This aircraft joined the flight development programme when it made its maiden flight on 28 October 1994, and was followed on 11 November by WA005, which was dedicated to testing the in-flight entertainment system and other avionics.

WA004 was allocated to general testing, as by the middle of December Boeing and the FAA had still not reached agreement on what truly represented an airline production aircraft, although the basic certification programme was on schedule for completion in April 1995.

ABOVE: During the flight development programme Boeing and customer airline engineers were able to prove the techniques for the maintenance of the aircraft in commercial service, checking accessibility. *Boeing*

Part of this certification was the better than expected noise levels which helped the 777 qualify for the demanding Stage 3 requirements: the engine operation was so quiet, that a significant proportion of the noise was caused by the airframe. The 1,000-flight ETOPS testing with the PW4084-powered aircraft finally began on 29 December 1994, almost two months later than planned, and in an effort to catch up lost time, up to 12 sorties a

day were being flown. By this stage Boeing had completed more than 540 test flights and over 1,430 hours on the first five PW4084-powered aircraft, with the first GE90-engined 777, N77779/G-ZZZA destined for British Airways, joining the programme on 2 February 1995. The first flight went very well, taking 5hr 20min, at altitudes up to 25,000ft and speeds of 250kts (460km/h). The GE90 engines, which were certificated to 85,000lb (380kN), used 76,050lb (340kN) for take-off at a gross weight of around 85,636lb (188,400kg). This success was marred by an emergency landing by WA002 at Boeing Field, caused by a sudden cabin-depressurisation, which

had to descend rapidly from 43,000ft (13,100m) during a test flight. Within a short time, on the same day, WA003 also suffered a depressurisation near Hawaii during a loads' survey flight test, and the FAA imposed a ceiling limit on all 777s of 25,000ft (7,620m), until a solution to the problem was found; this turned out to be a check valve failure in the air-conditioning system. This was corrected by 9 February, and approved by the FAA, allowing normal testing to resume.

The P&W ETOPS programme received a boost on 28 January when the 3,000-cycle endurance testing was successfully completed in the test-cell, which represented

up to six years of normal airline operation. This was being backed up by another which was flying on the ETOPS aircraft, which had run for 2,000 ground-based cycles before being installed in the aircraft. Rolls-Royce achieved certification of the Trent 800 from the FAA and JAA in January 1995 at 90,000lb (400kN) thrust with testing on the flight-test bed starting in March.

The GE90-powered 777 reached Mach 0.96 during a shallow dive in February 1995, ahead of schedule in the programme to expand the airframe/engine flight envelope. By the end of the first month of flight testing, the aircraft had flown around 40 hours and reached an altitude of 43,000ft (13,000m). Meanwhile total time on the PW4084-powered fleet exceeded 2,230 hours in 2,620 flights. The Trent 890 engine for the 777 made its first flight on the 747 test-bed on 29 March 1995, and was so successful that the planned 15-hour programme was cut to 12 hours. During this initial flight, which lasted 4hr 15min, the aircraft was taken up to 35,000ft (11,000m) and speeds of up to Mach 0.83, and amongst the tests were some high angle of attack manoeuvres. On the two further planned flights, tests included flights up to 43,000ft (13,106m), full power 90,000lb (400kN) thrust take-offs, re-lights, and slam accelerations and decelerations. As part of the ETOPS validation programme for the PW4084 engine, United began its month-long service-ready flights on 1 April 1995, within the overall 1,000-cycle programme. Boeing pilots retained command authority, but the aircraft was flown and serviced by United personnel.

ABOVE: The Boeing 777 proved to be very docile on the approach, with adequate flaps and good ground operation with the six-wheeled main undercarriage units. *Boeing*

ABOVE RIGHT: The flight-test progamme at Edwards included landing on a wet runway to check the aircraft's capability of landing in adverse weather, particularly that it did not aquaplane. *Boeing*

BELOW RIGHT: A similar test was conducted on the first production 777 for United. A pond was built on a taxiway at the Boeing facility at Glasgow, Montana, and the aircraft taxied through the water at various speeds, to satisfy the FAA. Boeing 777 WA002 N7772, later N774UA, was used extensively in the flight development programme, and was delivered to United on 29 March 1996. *Boeing*

On 19 April 1995 the Boeing 777 became the first US airliner to receive simultaneous type design and production certificates from both the US and European authorities. By the time the first aircraft was delivered to United, the overall certification effort reached around 3,300 hours, which compared with 1,800 hours on the 767 at the same stage. When certification was awarded, the seven aircraft in the flight development programme had flown more than 1,600 flights, and the eventual flight-test programme involving all nine aircraft was expected to cover 4,800 flights and over 6,700 hours. Following the initial certification, flight-test work continued on a range of improvements including the electronic check list and a thrust-asymmetry compensation (TAC) system, to take loads off the controls in the case of an engine failure. Flying also continued towards the achievement of ETOPS in time for the entry into service with

United, which was awarded by the FAA on 30 May 1995, just one week before revenue services started on 7 June. Meanwhile the JAA was only considering up to 120-minute ETOPS and specifying 50,000 engine hours of acceptable in-service operation, before giving 180 minutes' clearance for the 777/GE90 combination. The GE90 ETOPS approval 777 made its first flight on 16 May, but a surge had occurred on the first British Airways 777 during normal testing on 4 May, and an investigation was in hand to determine the cause. This was followed by a fan balance problem encountered

LEFT: In addition to the flight tests from the hot California desert at Edwards AFB, the Boeing 777 had to prove that it could also operate in extreme cold temperatures. The third aircraft, and the second for United, WA003 N7773 was the first 777 to visit Europe, flying to Kiruna in Northern Sweden in November 1994. This aircraft had joined the flight-test programme on 2 August 1994. Temperatures of down to -7°F (-21°C) were experienced, allowing validation of the cabin air conditioning and temperature control system. This aircraft was eventually delivered to United as N771UA on 27 November 1995. *Boeing*

BELOW LEFT: The Boeing-owned development 777, N7771 was used for the bulk of the flight development programme, sharing the flying with eight other production 777s. The No 1 aircraft shows the 777s generous wing area as vapour trails form behind the hot engine exhaust. *Boeing*

BELOW: The Boeing 777 flight development programme was a success. The first aircraft made its maiden flight on 12 June 1994, and the first delivery was to United Airlines on 17 May 1995 ready for revenue service to commence between London and Washington DC on 7 June. *Boeing*

during ground-running of the GE90, resulting in a precautionary grounding of the aircraft/engine combination from 24 May. These ground tests included the ingestion of a 3.6kg bird, and the engine passed the test successfully on 7 July, allowing test flying to recommence on 16 July, after nearly two months on the ground.

Further delays to the GE90 achieving ETOPS were caused in late 1995, when an engine surged during a pre-delivery test flight on a BA aircraft; although it recovered automatically there was some damage to the fan-rub strip and fan blades. As a result the formal ETOPS testing — expected to take up to four months — did not start until 30 March 1996, the original approval having been due in September 1995. The 777/GE90 combination completed the ETOPS flying on 31 July, with FAA approval due in mid-September after evaluation of the results.

The first Rolls-Royce Trent-powered 777 made its maiden flight on 26 May 1995 in the colours of Cathay Pacific, although initial commercial operations were started with Thai. During this 5hr 15min flight, the aircraft reached an altitude of 33,000ft (10,000m) and a speed of 365kt, (675km/h). Included in the tests were engine relights and slam accelerations and decelerations. However, during inspections following this otherwise successful flight, structural cracks were found in the aerodynamic fairing, which grounded the aircraft until it was

strengthened and commenced flying again on 1 July. The fairings on the P&W and GE engines were also checked by Boeing, who had responsibility for these parts, which do not carry any structural load.

Trent ETOPS testing started in early 1996, and by the end of February nearly 200 of the total of 1,000 cycles had been successfully flown. One of the two Trent-powered 777s was also flown on 91 of the Cathay route sectors, and returned to Seattle to continue Boeing trials. On 28 February 1996, the Boeing 777/Trent-engined variant was awarded FAA and JAA type certificates after a test effort involving more than 550 hours in over 180 flights. The Trent also became the world's most powerful engine at a thrust of 90,000lb (400kN). A delay was caused on 16 June 1996 when an engine surge on take-off caused an abort. Up to that time the ETOPS testing had been progressing well with some 886 cycles completed, representing nearly 90 percent of the estimated 1,008 required to achieve clearance. The surged engine was removed for investigation and was found to have suffered from foreign object damage; another well-used Trent was substituted on the test aircraft. The FAA approval for 180 minutes ETOPS with the 777/Trent 892 combination was finally awarded in early April 1997, in time for the first Trent-powered 777-200IGW delivery to Emirates.

On 3 August 1996 the 90,000lb (400kN) thrust PW4090 engine commenced a flight-test programme, fitted on the Boeing-owned first development aircraft, WA001. This engine was destined for the 777-200IGW aircraft for Korean and United and due to enter service in March 1997. The test programme was expected to involve up to 150 flight hours, and concentrate on the basic engine operating performance.

The first Rolls-Royce Trent-powered 777-200IGW made its first flight from Everett on 21 November 1996, eventually destined for Emirates after achieving ETOPS approval. Eight 777-200IGWs were allocated to the flight-test programme, with the three versions of the engines, the total flight time expected to be 775 hours. The first delivery of a -200IGW was planned to be a Pratt & Whitney-powered aircraft to United in March 1997. Certification of the Trent-powered aircraft was planned for March 1997, with deliveries to follow soon after.

Meanwhile, by mid-March 1997, the full-scale fatigue test airframe had undergone 120,000 simulated flights since January 1995, representing double the aircraft's 30-year service life, without any significant cracking. The airframe was then thoroughly inspected and high stress areas checked for fatigue in the structure.

RIGHT: The 777 flight tests formed one of the most comprehensive development programmes ever. By 11 April 1995 the flight-test fleet had flown more than 3,000 hours and completed some 4,000 hours of ground testing. In the first 10 months of test flying, the initial 777 was used for flutter tests to assess structural response at high speeds; low altitude ground effect tests to evaluate the handling qualities; minimum take-off speed tests and brake tests; stability and control tests; and 'configuration deviation list' tests to ensure that aerodynamic performance and handling qualities were not disrupted when various components are removed. *Boeing*

34

3 PRODUCTION

By mid-1992, two years before the Boeing 777 was due to make its maiden flight, the production programme was well established. This programme involved over 40 major suppliers, risk-sharing partners and sub-contractors in more than a dozen countries, as well as the smaller specialist suppliers. As Boeing issued the product definition, parts were starting to arrive, with about 35 percent of the computer-generated or data sets issued to the suppliers. The aim was to release some 90 percent of the data to suppliers by the spring of 1993, when the first major sub-assemblies were to be started in the jigs.

The production plan outlined at the start was based on the following main principles which allowed the design to be market-driven: design to be complete before production started; design/build teams to be used to ensure a concurrent engineering capability; and a service-ready aircraft to be produced. During 1992, to remain on programme, Boeing had to release the design data to the suppliers, as well as to Boeing's own manufacturing organisation, followed in 1993 with start of major assembly at the beginning of the year, and also commis-

sioning of the systems integration laboratory (SIL). The innovative SIL, one of many firsts for Boeing in the 777 programme, is basically a complete aircraft without its skin and is part of a $90 million investment by Boeing in an overall integrated air-

RIGHT: The stringers are attached to the wing-skins using a sophisticated new automated fastening machine. The machine is capable of precision installation of more than 28 different rivets, bolts or nuts at the rate of six every minute. With more than 17,000 fasteners in each main wing skin, the machine completes a panel in about three days. *Boeing*

BELOW RIGHT: Fuselage sections are built inverted, keel upwards, for improved accessibility during production, and then rotated in a special turning fixture for completion of the top side. The forward cabin section weighs around 14,000lb (6,356kg) when removed for completion, and the section turning takes about 20 minutes. *Boeing*

BELOW: The vast wide-bodied jet production facility at Everett, where Boeing 747s, 767s and 777s are assembled, each on their separate lines. Included in this facility are the computer-controlled paint-shops, where precisely the right thickness of paint is applied to protect the aircraft, without increasing the weight more than necessary. Production flight-testing of the wide-bodied jet airliners is from this site, and a number of 747s can be seen being completed outside before flight test, acceptance and delivery. *Boeing*

craft systems laboratory. This new systems laboratory opened in the autumn of 1992, and brought together up to 26 laboratories and support units in the Puget Sound area around Seattle, allowing Boeing to develop and integrate the aircraft systems in a more systematic manner. In particular, the SIL is able to test and validate all the electric and electronic interface messages throughout the many 777 systems. Unlike previous aircraft, the Boeing 777 required a high level of integration, which made the overall systems testing more important using representative equipment, to ensure that there were no delays to the flight test schedule.

The 757 systems test-rig was used to test the initial flight control architecture and prototype hardware, while the dedicated 777 flight-control test-rig was being built in the new integrated aircraft systems laboratory. The new flight-control rig was complete with flight-control surfaces, the fly-by-wire control system, full electrical systems and major parts of the hydraulics. To test the 777 control laws, and the philosophy behind them, a production 757 was equipped with a switchable dual autopilot. The 777 development autopilot incorporated new software from Rockwell-Collins representing the normal control laws, to allow checking of the control feel, behaviour of the system and ensure that its operation was instinctive.

As would be expected in such a complex aircraft, there were a number of design changes during the early development, but most were dealt with before the critical design reviews commenced. All major changes were incorporated into the computerised design in preparation for the final stages of digital pre-assembly (DPA). Most of the DPA and design definition was completed on schedule by the end of March 1992, but further work between the design/build teams on completion of the design resulted in this phase continuing until the end of July.

An early design change to allow the shorter-range A-model to fly internationally, was the increase of the gross weight from 512,600lb (233,000kg) to 533,940 (242,700kg). The A-model range was therefore increased from 5,000 miles (7,960km) to 5,600 miles (9,020km). This also brought the A-model closer to the take-off weight of the B-model at 589,820lb (268,100kg), giving a range of 7,300 miles (11,750km).

RIGHT: Once rotated the wing is pressure-tested to ensure that there will be no fuel leaks. When this has been established, the painting process follows. The equipping includes systems installation, hydraulics, fuel piping and electrical wiring. *Boeing*

BELOW: The structurally complete port wing, weighing around 14 tons (14,200kg) is lifted out of the assembly jig and laid flat on the floor mounted cradle supports where internal and external equipping is completed. Each 90ft (27.4m) long wing is then joined to the fuselage centre section before final assembly. *Boeing*

Airlines not requiring the higher gross weight options will not suffer performance penalties, as the empty weight remains the same — a result of the success of the overall weight reduction programme. Since the start of design in 1991, the weight had been reduced by 15,000lb (6,800kg) in mid 1992, with a further 1,000lb (455kg) as the ultimate target.

Because of the need by All Nippon to have some additional length on the A-model to provide more capacity on the short dense Japanese domestic routes, two more fuselage frames were added, with the agreement of United, the launch customer, taking the overall length to 209ft (63.7m).

In addition to the weight reduction programme, initial laboratory evaluations, wind tunnel testing and better than predicted fuel consumption from the engine manufacturers' gave a high level of confidence in advance that the 777 would enter service within its predicted performance guarantees. The digital pre-assembly has helped with some modest weight reductions, due to avoiding duplication of parts, the results being reviewed by the DBTs. To prove the new CATIA design system in practice, a nose section was built and the assembly of the many components was tested, to check that they would fit according to the computer predictions. The nose section was chosen as it is the most densely packed part of the aircraft and it allowed a practical evaluation for maintenance access, as well as an evaluation of engineering human factors in the fitting of the systems.

Structural testing started with a 21ft (6.4m) long fuselage section for initial pressure testing; and a 44ft (13.4m) tailplane, similar to a scaled-up version of the 767 tailplane, but mainly made from composites, which was tested to in excess of two predicted life cycles of the aircraft. The major structural test specimens were two complete airframes, one for static testing, and the other for the longer term fatigue testing. The aim with the test specimens was to ensure that the predicted life of 40,000 cycles was achieved, testing continuing to cover 44,000 cycles to provide an ample margin.

As part of the service-ready initiative, Boeing provided the suppliers with more defined performance and functional requirements than previously. They were then validated by analysis and simulation, the results becoming the basis for the systems design requirement and objectives document, with a systems development plan for each component. By providing each supplier with a flow chart showing how the part was to be designed, developed and tested, and the interfaces with the adjacent systems, each contractor had sufficient information to design and build all the parts that worked together. Many of the major suppliers worked with Boeing on the design/build teams to ensure achieving the final requirements, each company contributing design, development or manufacturing expertise, providing a significant benefit to all parties. In mid-1992 there were still nearly 330 DBTs active on the 777 programme.

The widely dispersed production of the 777 airframe, engines, systems and equipment created many logistical challenges, both within North America, and overseas. Boeing is

LEFT: The forward fuselage from the front pressure bulkhead to the wing centre-section is assembled as one piece. *Boeing*

responsible for a major portion of the structure, including the forward fuselage, known as Section 41, the wingbox, fixed leading edges, wing trailing edge panels, composite tailfin and composite tailplane. The composite tail-sections are produced at a new Boeing facility at Frederickson, south of Seattle, and the first set came out at less than the predicted cost — but Boeing wanted costs reduced further, to the equivalent or less than building them with aluminium. Savings were also anticipated from a challenging programme of reducing flow times from 123 days per aircraft set at the start in April 1993, to 38 days in 1997. The use of composites in the tail assemblies reduces weight by 1,650lb (750kg), which represents 78 miles (125km) extra range, and gives an appropriate parts reduction of 777.

The Boeing Wichita factory is responsible for the manufacture of pylons, cowlings and nacelles for all three engine types selected to power the 777. The first pylon was delivered to Boeing for installation on the Boeing 747 testbed for the flight testing of the Pratt & Whitney PW4000 series engine. Wichita also has responsibility for the aluminium seat-tracks, the corrosion-resistant titanium for the galley and toilet areas being subcontracted to United Engineering.

Grumman Aerostructures in the USA have responsibility for the wing spoilers and inboard flaps, in a subcontract worth at least $570 million over the first 10 years. Grumman already had the experience of producing the smaller composite spoilers for the 757, the first set for the 777 being delivered in September 1993. Grumman had not produced flaps for a large airliner before, but used its experience with the McDonnell Douglas C-17 ailerons as a basis for the winning bid for the 777 work, which will be worth around $450 million. Each 22ft (6.7m) long carbon-fibre inboard flap consists of the main and aft surfaces.

The wing trailing edge structure is being built by Kaman Aerospace, who already supply similar parts for the 767. In the case of the 777, a newly developed Aluminium 7000 toughened alloy is used for the machined and assembled parts, the first set of hardware being delivered to Boeing in February 1993. The North American Aircraft Division of Rockwell International is responsible for the carbonfibre composite floor beams and the aluminium wing leading edge slats. This Tulsa-based facility is contracted to produce 500 ship-sets of 74 beams per aircraft with the first delivery in December 1993. The first set of 14 leading edge slats were delivered in October 1993.

A number of other structural components were supplied from US companies, including the exhaust cowling assembly, and thermal barriers in the engine nacelles.

Japan is a major overseas risk-sharing partner in the 777 programme with around 20 percent of the aircraft being built by Mitsubishi, Kawasaki and Fuji Heavy Industries. They are formed into the Japan Aircraft Development Corporation (JADC) and are responsible for significant sections of the fuselage and wings. JADC, together with subcontractors Japan Aircraft Manufacturing and Shina Meiwa Industry, participated in the Boeing DBTs. The Japanese industry is responsible for most of the fuselage panels and all the doors, wing centre-section, wing to fuselage fairings and wing ribs between the spars. The wing ribs were the first items to be delivered in April 1993, followed by the first fuselage panels in June, the initial set of doors in August and the wing to fuselage fairings in November. The significant contribution made by Japan to the 777, and therefore the dollars earned, makes the airliner a more cost effective buy for the national airlines.

About 200 Japanese engineers were based in Seattle in early 1992 to work with the DBTs, before returning to their own country to oversee the production of the parts. Mitsubishi had the largest Japanese share of the 777 with the manufacture of the rear fuselage panels, representing about 40 percent of the Japanese total. In a new specially built factory at Nagoya, Kawasaki is producing the forward and centre fuselage panels, wing between spar ribs and bulkhead, accounting for about 30 percent of the Japanese workshare. Fuji is responsible for the wing centre-section and main undercarriage doors, having built a new final assembly factory at Handa, near Nagoya, on the coast, to make the shipping by sea easier. The Japanese investment in the 777 is therefore significant at around $870 million for the development, and half as much again in new buildings and tools.

Other overseas suppliers of structural components include Alenia of Italy, which has been awarded a £300 million contract for the radome and outboard wing flaps, having gained experience with Boeing in the past in the manufacture of composite components. Korean Air make parts of the wingtip and the flap support fairings under a contract worth $100 million, and Embraer of Brasil is involved with elements of the wingtip assembly and the dorsal fin. Short Bros of Northern Ireland and Singapore Aerospace share the supply of the nose undercarriage doors. Major suppliers are also located in Australia: AeroSpace Technologies of Australia (ASTA) is responsible for the rudder manufacture, one of the largest all-composite primary structures used to date on any Boeing airliner. The rudder is 33ft (10.2m) tall and weighs 315lb (143kg). Hawker de Havilland, also in Australia, manufacture the 33ft 10in (10.3m) long composite elevators, the first rudder and elevators being delivered to Boeing in October 1993, a year after commencement of manufacture.

In addition to the obvious supply of the engines, filling the airframe is a considerable amount of equipment developed by many specialist companies from a number of countries, as well as from the USA. Amongst the most significant items on the equipment list is the APU, in the case of the 777 being the Allied Signal Aerospace Garrett GCTP 331-500. Essential for the compliance for ETOPS from service entry, the APU had to be extremely reliable, and the first unit was run by March 1992. The aim was to achieve 3,000 hours of running during the first year of testing, building up to 10,000 hours of operation by the time the 777 was certificated in 1994, an increase of

ABOVE RIGHT: Great care has to be taken when lowering the fuselage sections into the assembly jig to not only avoid damage to this large section, but also to ensure that it is correctly supported avoiding any distortion. *Boeing*

RIGHT: Once the wings are equipped and fitted with the engine pylons, they are joined to the fuselage centre-section. They are then lifted out of the jig ready to join the other fuselage sections in the final assembly. *Boeing*

ABOVE: With the tail components in place, and the special fixture around the fuselage joining, the Boeing 777 is surrounded by staging to give access to all parts of the aircraft. *Boeing*

ABOVE LEFT: The wing centre-section is lowered into place in the final assembly jig. Precise positioning is achieved by using a computer operated laser alignment and levelling system. The sections are then permanently fastened followed by the completion of the systems installation and the fitting of the landing gear, wing flaps and fairings. *Boeing*

BELOW LEFT: The rear cabin is lowered into position following the wing centre-section to allow the final assembly process to commence, all this takes around four weeks. *Boeing*

40 percent over any previous APU testing. The running of the first three development APUs was well advanced by mid-1992, followed by the fourth unit, which ran 3,200 hours with 12,800 starts as part of the endurance testing. The cold soak testing was done in Alaska, to ensure starting under all conditions.

The central hydraulic system is driven by an Garrett Fluid Systems air drive unit which is powered by the APU, a ground power unit, or more normally in the air by engine bleed air. Since the start of development it now delivers 45 percent more power, it has unlimited life and it offers a high level of redundancy. Allied Signal's AirResearch Division is responsible for the cabin pressure and air supply systems, the integrated system controller, ozone converter — which removes contaminants, electronics bay heating and the ram-air turbine.

Hamilton Standard has developed the cabin air-conditioning and temperature control system. The air-conditioning system, of which two packs are supplied for each aircraft, uses for the first time a lighter, easily maintained condensing cycle technology, and a single pack demonstrated ice-free operations in all conditions, giving systems redundancy. Hamilton Standard also produced the wing and engine-cowling ice protection systems, the latter being delivered to the engine manufacturers in April 1993.

The primary electrical power generation system and its variable speed, constant frequency (VSCF) back-up was developed by Sundstrand Electric Power Systems. The primary system comprises two engine-driven integrated drive generators, an APU-driven generator, with generator and bus-power control units. In the unlikely event of the primary system failing, the VSCF provides back-up AC power for all the aircraft instrumentation, pumps, fans and lighting. Separate generators on each engine, independent of the primary system, provide redundant power sources for the single back-up converter. Ground testing of the complete system started in April 1994. Sundstrand also supplied the ground proximity warning system for the 777.

The distinctive six-wheel main landing gear and the traditional nose gear are both produced by Canadian-based Menasco Aerospace, together with its French partner, Messier-Bugatti. The 14 ft 6in (4.4m) high main gear is built at the Menasco factory in Dallas, Texas and at Bidos in France, the first of 500 contracted ship-sets being delivered in August 1993. Another first for Boeing on the 777 was the offer of a choice of wheels and brakes, between B. F. Goodrich and Bendix. The B. F. Goodrich wheels and brakes were developed from the ones used on the Boeing 747-400, but with an increased thermal capacity to allow for quicker turn-rounds. The brakes are made from the proven Supercarb carbon-carbon composite brake-disc/heat-sink material, protected from radiating heat and contaminants by a perforated stainless-steel ring. The Bendix Wheels and Brakes Division of Allied Signal is offering Carbenix, a new carbon brake material which gives improved disc strength, dynamic stability and oxidation resistance. The Bendix wheels have encapsulated bearings to retain the lubricant over the longer tyre lives now being experienced.

Goodyear bias-ply tyres are standard for the main wheels, but Michelin radial tyres are standard on the nose-wheel, and an option for the main wheels. This is the first time that a US commercial jet airliner has been certificated with radial tyres as standard, the weight saving being around 20 percent over bias tyres.

THE FLIGHTDECK

The flightdeck and its systems are an essential part of the aircraft, and the 777 has a number of advanced features. The brains of the aircraft is the integrated management system (AIMS) and the integrated air-data/inertial reference system, which are both supplied by Honeywell. The AIMS provides central processing and input/output hardware to perform flight management, display symbology generation, central maintenance, aircraft condition monitoring, digital communications management and data conversion. Amongst the challenges involved in the development of these systems were the non-reflective glass for the active-matrix liquid-crystal flat-panel displays, and active avionics cooling to meet the requirements of extended-range operations.

Within the AIMS, Honeywell also developed the graphics computer for the primary flight instruments (the EFIS and the engine-indication and crew alerting system) using flat panel displays for improved reliability, lower weight and less power. The 777 was the first commercial application for this technology, the displays needing to be clear over wide viewing angles, allowing one crew member, to look across the flight deck, and see the other pilot's displays.

The autopilot, maintenance access terminal and the standby instruments have all been developed by Rockwell-Collins. The Triplex redundant autopilot has been especially developed for the 777 and as the aircraft has fly-by-wire controls, a back-drive system was developed to move the control yoke in response to autopilot commands. The AIMS maintenance terminal has 8x8in (20x20cm) full colour liquid crystal displays, with a keyboard and disc loaders, used to programme up to 50 onboard systems, using a fibre-optic avionics network.

ABOVE: The first three 777s for United seen completing systems installation and cabin furnishing, prior to the fitting of the engines followed by painting. The rudders are always painted in advance to ensure correct balance. The third aircraft is close to being rolled out of the assembly jig. *Boeing*

LEFT: Once it is structurally complete, the Boeing 777 is pulled out from the assembly jig on its own undercarriage for the completion of systems installation. *Boeing*

The primary flight control computers (PFCC) were developed by GEC Avionics in Britain, the programme progressing smoothly. The first fly-by-wire computers were delivered to Boeing in early May for installation in the 757 iron bird test-rig, and operated as required. Each 777 has three PFCCs, which drive 12 power control units (PCU) on the major control surfaces via four actuator control electronics (ACE) boxes. The PCUs are being supplied by Teijin Seiki of Japan and has teamed with Lear Astronics to produce the ACEs.

Allied Signal Aerospace developed the 30 ship-set leading-edge geared rotary activators; Moog supplied the activators for the spoilers and Parker-Bertea provided the primary activators for the elevators. The trim control module and the secondary hydraulic brake for the tailplane were developed by E-Systems, whose Montek Division was responsible for the optional folding wingtip.

The Dowty Group in Britain supplies the thrust reverser actuation system for all three engine combinations, wing leading-edge power drive unit and offset gearboxes, and the nose-gear door and main undercarriage uplock actuators and hydraulic fuses. The hydraulic superfuses are designed to detect leaks and automatically seal off fluid flow. The electrical load management and fuel quantity indicating systems were also developed in Britain by Smiths Industries. The fuel quantity indicating system uses 50 ultra-sonic sensors in each fuel tank, presenting the data on the flight-deck displays.

The initial production plans called for six 777s per month from the Everett facility, which would equate to 350 aircraft by the year 2000. Assembly of the first 777 started in early 1993 with the nose-wheel well installation in the lower forward fuselage section. This particular structure was made from aluminium and titanium, and assembled using numerically controlled equipment. By August of the same year, the first major fuselage section and the port wing were completed at Everett. Despite 1993 being a bad year for airliner deliveries, due to the continuing economic depression, the production rate of the 777 was maintained, while other programmes were reduced to match demand. Some lay-offs of employees were

47

unavoidable, 17,000 departing in 1993, followed by a further 7,000 in 1994, but the 777 boosted revenues when deliveries commenced in 1995.

By end November 1993 the front fuselage for the first 777 was in final assembly; the following month the fuselage centre-section, and rear fuselage were joined, making the first aircraft 90 percent structurally complete. At the roll-out of the first 777 on 9 April 1994, the second aircraft, the first for United, was structurally complete and in an advanced stage of equipping.

With the first aircraft complete at the roll-out, work then commenced on the testing of the key systems, and checking for any last minute software faults. An intense effort was concentrated in three major areas — the flight-control system (FCS) software, engine integration and AIMS software. To ensure the integrity of the FCS required between 500 and 600 hours of critical tests in the iron bird supplemented by further testing in the SILs. Much of the testing was concentrated on the primary flight computers, to evaluate safety, performance and maintainability, particularly under more demanding conditions. Pratt & Whitney had to compress the engine delivery schedule, following a failure during early testing, the first two flight engines being delivered by the end of April. By early May, 92 percent of the AIMS software was delivered, to allow initial flight trials, the full airline standard being achieved in September ready for the start of accelerated ETOPS development.

FIRST FLIGHT

Finally the day came for the maiden flight of this largest of twin-engined jet airliners, on 12 June 1994, when the first aircraft lifted off for its 3 hour 48 minute flight with 777 Chief Pilot John Cashman and Ken Higgins, director of flight test, in control. This was the first of what was expected to be about 4,800 test flights, leading to initial certification in April 1995, and first delivery to United on 15 May.

With the improving world economy in 1996, and following a Boeing production workers' strike, the 777 production rate was planned to rise to 3.5 aircraft in the second half of the year, moving to a planned steady rate of five a month from early 1997, the maximum rate being seven a month, which was achieved in July.

The first 777-200 increased gross weight (IGW) for British Airways started assembly on 20 February 1996, for delivery to the airline in early 1997. Assembly of the stretched 777-300 commenced in late March 1997, with the roll-out planned for August, followed by the first flight in October, the planned production rate for this version being up to 28 a year by 2002. Building of the 777 family is therefore well established, with senior Boeing executives predicting an overall production life of up to 50 years.

LEFT: Engine development continues to support the demands of improved performance for the increased range and higher power of each new variant of the Boeing 777. All the engines are of similar large size, this example being the Rolls-Royce Trent fitted to a SIA 777, the mechanic providing scale. *Rolls-Royce*

BELOW LEFT: In the vast new specially constructed Boeing 777 assembly hall at Everett, aircraft are in the final stages of completion for United, Cathay Pacific, British Airways and All Nippon. *Boeing*

BELOW: The first Boeing 777 was unveiled on 9 April 1994 to a total of nearly 100,000 people representing Boeing employees, customers programme partners, suppliers, sub-contractors and engine company representatives. To accommodate so many people, they were introduced at about 7,000 at a time in 15 presentations and the customer airline logos were projected on screens behind the aircraft. *Boeing*

4 TECHNICAL SPECIFICATION

	777-200	777-200IGW	777-300	777-200X	777-300X
Dimensions					
Span *ft.in (m)*	199.9 (60.9)	199.9 (60.9)	199.9 (60.9)	204.4 (62.28)	204.4(62.28)
Length *ft.in (m)*	209.1 (63.7)	209.1 (63.7)	242 4 (73.8)	209.1 (63.7)	242.1 (73.8)
Height *ft.in (m)*	60.4 (18.4)	60.4 (18.4)	60.4 (18.4)	60.4 (18.4)	60.4 (18.4)
Wing area *sq ft(sq m)*	460.5 (42.8)	460.5 (42.8)	460.5 (42.8)		
Sweep *degrees*	31.6	31.6	31.6	31.6	31.6
Landing gear					
Track *ft in (m)*	36.1 (11)	36.1 (11)	36.1 (11)	(11)	36.1 (11)
Wheelbase *ft in (m)*	84.7 (25.8)	84.7 (25.8)	102.2 (31.14)	84.7 (25.8)	102 2 (31.14)
Turn radius *ft in (m)*	134.6 (41)	134.6 (41)		134.6 (41)	
Accommodation					
Max seats	440	440	550	298	355
Weights *lb (kg)*					
Max t/o	504,900 (229,500)	588,720 (267,600)	572,000 (260,000)	709,148 (322,340)	
Zero fuel	419,100 (190,500)	429,110 (195,050)			
Fuel *US gal (litres)*	30,508 (117,340)	43,992 (169,200)			
Payload range					
Max *lb (kg)*	119,790 (54,450)	119,790 (54,450)			
Range *miles (km)*	3,390 (5,460)	5,750 (9,260)	6,334 (10,200)	9,873 (15,900)	7,576 (12,200)
Full tanks wt *lb (kg)*	74,844 (34,020)	63,910 (29,050)			
Range *miles(km)*	5,290 (8,520)	8,110 (13,060)			
FAR field length at gross weight (m)					
Take-off	7,003 (2,135)	8,791 (2,680)			
Landing	5,281 (1,610)	5,609 (1,710)			
Speeds *kts*					
V AT	138	140			
V NO	330	330			
Cruise					
Max cruise speed *kts*	499	499			
Altitude *ft in (m)*	11,887 (39,000)	11,887 (39,000)			
Long range speed *kts*	476	476			
Altitude *ft in (m)*	11,887 (39,000)	11,887 (39,000)			

ABOVE RIGHT: United 777s are now regular and familiar visitors to London Heathrow. The service introduction of the high technology aircraft went generally smoothly, living up to the 'service ready' claims demanded by the airlines. N770UA WA013, which first flew as N77772 on 26 June 1995 and was delivered on 12 July, is seen ready for departure from London Heathrow in April 1997. *Philip Birtles*

RIGHT: The first 777 delivered to BA at London Heathrow, was G-ZZZC WA015 on 12 November 1995. It entered service on 17 November on routes to Dubai and Muscat. *BA*

FUSELAGE

The 777 was the first Boeing airliner designed from the inside out, starting with the passenger cabin before any of the other structures. This may appear logical, since the cabin is what the airlines sell, but it is rarely the first thing designed. The circular-section fuselage allowed twin-aisle seating layouts, from six-abreast in First Class to 10-abreast in Economy Class. The 777 was one of the first Boeing airliners to have a circular cross-section fuselage, which gave greater simplicity and less weight, plus was easier to build. For the developed, stretched and higher all-up weight versions of the 777, considerable strengthening was required in the fuselage centre-section to overcome the additional bending loads.

To cope with the greater fatigue and fracture strength requirements of the fuselage skin, Boeing selected a newly developed aluminium alloy by Alcoa called 2XXX; it was also used in the fabrication of the large aft-pressure dome at the rear of the cabin. For the fuselage stringers, Boeing selected stronger 7150 alloy extrusions, with a Z-section, which avoids corrosion from trapped moisture or condensation. The 7150 alloy is also more corrosion resistant, and is especially useful for the fuselage structure, where fluid spillage is an occupational hazard. In addition to the stringers, the fuselage skins are reinforced by frames spaced on average 20in (50cm) apart. The skins are also machined, or where there are complicated shapes, they are chemically milled, to remove material for weight saving where less structural strength is required. As well as transferring loads to the skin, the function of the frames, is to maintain the cross sectional shape of the fuselage.

Traditionally, the worst area for corrosion in a fuselage is under the floors below the galleys, toilets, and sometimes the seats, where fluids are spilled and then seep through. In the past, Boeing engineers have ensured a suitable corrosion protection under the galleys and toilets, but with the flexibility of the 777 cabin layout, corrosion protection became more of a challenge. Major customer-driven aspects of the 777 cabin were the large area flexible zones, within which the toilets and galleys could be relocated and easily plumbed in. This gave the airlines a rapid way to respond to passenger demand by reconfiguring the seating and class layouts. While First Class features a standard twin-aisle six-abreast layout, Business Class can be configured as seven-abreast (2-3-2), or eight-abreast (2-4-2), and Economy Class can be anything from nine-abreast (2-5-2) to 10-abreast (3-4-3). In the flex zones the seat tracks are made from titanium, the transverse floor beams supporting the seat tracks are produced from composites of carbon fibre and toughened resins, and they are attached to the fuselage frames by aluminium end fittings. The floor panels are made from a lightweight laminated sandwich of carbon fibre or glass-fibre reinforced plastic skins, with a Nomex aramid honeycomb core.

RIGHT: The 777 cabin was designed from the inside out, allowing seat layouts from six abreast to 10 abreast, while still leaving the aisles wide enough for passengers to pass during service from the cabin crews. From Top to Bottom — First Class cabin with roomy twin-aisle six-abreast layout. Business Class can be configured as seven-abreast (2-3-2), or eight-abreast (2-4-2), a typical seven-abreast being shown. Economy Class can be configured at nine-abreast in the 2-5-2 layout or 10-abreast in the 3-4-3 layout. *Boeing*

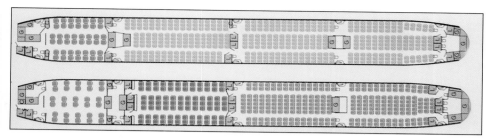

400 *passengers, two-class at 38-, 32-in pitch*

305 *passengers, three-class at 60-, 38-, 32-in pitch*

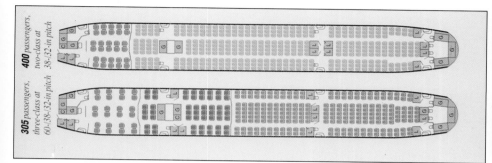

TOP LEFT: Various typical interior seating arrangements showing 777-300 above and 777-200 below. *Boeing*

TOP: The First Class cabin in Malaysian 777s is configured in the traditional 2-2-2 six-abreast seating layout. *MAS*

CENTRE LEFT: BA 777s have sky-phones located in the vestibule areas as well as in the seat arms. *Philip Birtles*

ABOVE: The 777s with Emirates have the latest technology in passenger entertainment and communications, including a sky phone in the seat-back. *Emirates*

LEFT: The galleys and toilets are capable of being located over a wide range of positions, to provide flexibility in the different cabin layouts. The forward galley installed in the ANA 777s has been designed to provide the highest standards of in-flight catering, even though the aircraft is only used on domestic services. *ANA*

USE OF COMPOSITES

Nearly 10 percent of the 777 structure is non-metallic, reducing weight and corrosion, the major structural areas being the tail surfaces. Composites are also used for wing trailing edge control surfaces, spoilers, fixed wing leading-edges, engine nacelles, wing to fuselage fairings, and main undercarriage doors. The use of composites saved 2,595lb (1,180kg) of structural weight, and the use of advanced aluminium saved a further 3,190lb (1,450kg). At the start of the 777 programme, it was always the intention to use the new lightweight aluminium lithium alloy wherever possible. However this was not possible due chipping of the metal when fasteners were used. This did not cause a structural problem, but was instead a quality control concern.

SECONDARY SUPPORT STRUCTURE

One of the benefits of the CATIA digital design and pre-assembly system was in the installation of the overhead bins for passenger carry-on luggage. They can hold up to 84lb (38kg) each, and on installation, it was found that almost every bin fitted exactly into place, saving 65 percent of rework and adjustment over previous cabins. The key to cabin flexibility was the secondary support structure, the cabin roof and bins being supported by an arch assembly, mounted on a pair of fore-and-aft rails. Large tie-rods supporting the arch transfer loads of up to 47,960lb (21,800kg) into the fuselage structure, and are stressed to 9g. Additional tie-rods and bracing structure support the ceiling. The seat-rails are also stressed to 9g, while the seats comply with the latest FAA 16g crash-loads. It was not easy to get agreement between the initial eight airlines, as to where the extremities of the flex zones should be, as it certainly added weight and complexity, but the toilets can now be relocated three hours, instead of up to two days in previous aircraft.

ABOVE: Great care was taken to ensure the overhead carry-on luggage bins were accessible, roomy and avoided dropping items on the passengers. *Philip Birtles*

ABOVE RIGHT: The advanced technology flightdeck of the Boeing 777 features flat panel displays. In the centre, above the twin engine power levers, is the engine indicating and crew alerting system (EICAS). The flat panels on either side, in front of each pilot, are the navigation/multifunction displays (ND/MFD), and outboard of them are the twin primary flight displays (PFD). A multifunction display is hidden behind the thrust levers, and on either side and the rear of the centre console are flight management control display units (CDU). *Boeing*

BELOW: United Airlines Boeing 777 Connoisseur Class is configured in a roomy 2-3-2 seven-abreast layout with easy access to the overhead baggage lockers. *United*

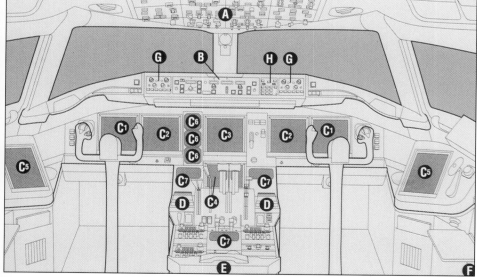

LEFT: *Key to drawing of flightdeck*
A. Overhead panel with larger nomenclature, cool LED-lighted switches and lightplates, and flightdeck lighting master brightness control.

B. Full-time, triple-channel autopilot mode control panel with new method of selecting flight path angle and track modes.

C. Colour flat-panel liquid crystal displays (LCDs) — 1 Primary flight displays, 2 Navigation/malfunction displays, 3 Engine indicating and crew alerting system, 4 Malfunction display, 5 optional side LCDs, 6 Standby flight instruments, 7 Flight management control displays.

D. Touch-pad cursor control devices.

E. Full-size printer.

F. Maintenance station.

G. Electronic flight instrument system control panel.

H. Display select panel.

The large fuselage cross-section also provides enormous cargo capacity, not only below deck, but also on the main floor. One of the options is a large cargo door, although the structural strengthening resulting from the large cut-out in the cabin, adds around 990lb (450kg) of weight. In terms of weight, there is more cargo capacity in a 777 than in the 747-400, but less volume; a planned fuselage stretch will mean the 777's under-floor cargo capacity will be the greater.

In the event of an extreme overload, the engine support strut is designed to separate from the wing, without damaging the wing-box structure. The engine strut is made from a mix of composites, titanium and aluminium sheet metal, the upper aft fairing covering the hydraulic systems. The strut contains fuel lines, hydraulic pipes, thrust reverser controls, fire extinguish-ers and engine controls. The Allied Signal auxiliary power unit (APU) located in the aft fuselage fairing, can be started at any part of the flight envelope, up to 43,000ft (13,106m), as well as on the ground, and will shut down automatically, in case of a major fault.

FLIGHTDECK CONFIGURATION

The flightdeck of the 777 is based on that established in the Boeing 747-400, combined with the 767 flightdeck. The 747-400 provided the latest electronics interface, and because the 777 was a twin-engined aircraft, it used the basic architecture of the 767 twin. As with the remainder of the aircraft, the concept of customer as partner was important, with nearly 600 aircrew from the airlines, regulatory authorities, vendors and industry

LEFT: On the starboard side of the flightdeck is the maintenance access terminal. This gives ground engineers access to systems serviceability when undertaking routine maintenance. *Boeing*

BELOW LEFT: The cabin air conditioning is managed by the cabin crew through a computer-controlled monitor just aft of the flight-deck. *Philip Birtles*

BELOW: Flightdeck layout. *Boeing*

BOTTOM: The MFD provides the crew with systems information and is located just forward of the twin thrust levers. On either side are the CDUs, and the pair of fairings on either side of the thrust levers are the mouse pads for selecting data on the screens. *Philip Birtles*

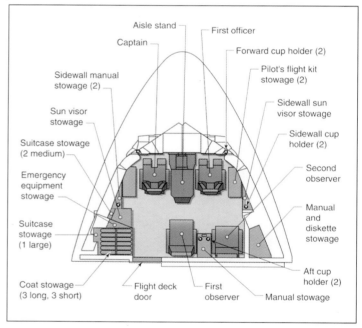

Aisle stand
First officer
Captain
Forward cup holder (2)
Sidewall manual stowage (2)
Pilot's flight kit stowage (2)
Sun visor stowage
Sidewall sun visor stowage
Suitcase stowage (2 medium)
Sidewall cup holder (2)
Emergency equipment stowage
Second observer
Suitcase stowage (1 large)
Manual and diskette stowage
Coat stowage (3 long, 3 short)
Flight deck door
First observer
Manual stowage
Aft cup holder (2)

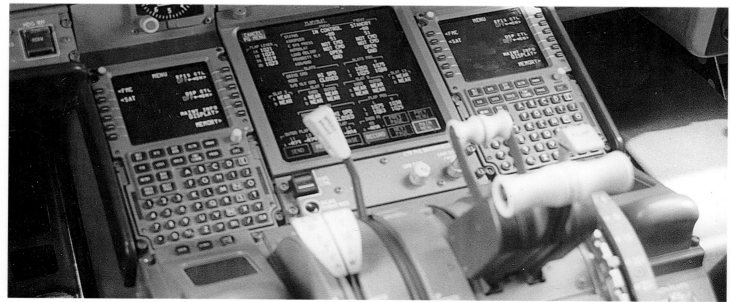

operating the engineering development simulators. Over 300 pilots flew 560 hours, added to more than 1,500 hours flown by 33 Boeing pilots, who were directly involved in the design, testing and evaluations in the systems integration laboratory and the flight-control test-rig. One of the major decisions to be made was whether to stay with the conventional control column or use a side stick controller, similar to that installed by Airbus. The decision was finally made in favour of continuing with the conventional control columns, to retain the normal feedback through the controls. This approach is maintained with the throttles, as even when they are operating under automatic control, they move according to the power setting.

The flightdeck has a crew of two who face six interchangeable flat panel Honeywell displays, arranged side-by-side, to give a clear view even when the pilots sit back. Two further observers' seats are located on the flightdeck, one having access to the maintenance terminal, to be used by ground engineers when downloading servicing data. In addition to the normal flight operational data on the cockpit displays, the check-lists are also included, ensuring all actions are achieved before moving on to the next item.

WINGS

The wing design follows the Boeing tradition of having a more than adequate area, allowing for plenty of future development, but it is also the most advanced aerofoil yet produced by Boeing, carrying more lift further aft than before. There is also a high angle of dihedral to give adequate ground clearance for the large underwing-podded engines. The thick supercritical wing shape is most obvious to inspection when viewed on the outboard undersides of the wing, where there is significant

BELOW: The big wing of the 777 with its large flaps and leading edge devices gives it docile handling qualities at low speeds on the approach. *Philip Birtles*

BOTTOM LEFT: To gain maximum efficiency and keep drag to a minimum Boeing had to attend to detail in the design of the 777. An example is the careful blending of the shape of the wing-root fairing around the leading edge, which also shows the highly efficient airfoil shape of the advanced wing, moving the centre of lift further aft, resulting in a thicker and lighter wing with more room for fuel. *Philip Birtles*

BOTTOM RIGHT: British Airways was the first airline to introduce the Boeing 777/GE90 engine combination to service, and it is also the first time that BA has ordered GE engines (BA inherited the CF6s in the DC-10s acquired from British Caledonian which are operated from Gatwick). The first engine change proved to be quite challenging, due to the large scale, but the engineering team has now become more accustomed to handling the units. *Philip Birtles*

inverse camber. The wing is optimised for a Mach 0.83 cruise, and would generate considerable additional drag if pushed beyond that speed.

The wings span almost 200ft (61m), with an area of around 4,628sq ft (430 sq m). The high aspect ratio of 8.68 of the wing allows adequate development, with the current maximum take-off weight of between 506,100lb (230,000kg) and 627,000lb (285,000kg), the latter representing the heaviest weight non-USA, or B-market aircraft. The current wing is probably limited to a maximum take-off weight of 720,000lb (327,000kg) because it has reached its ultimate wing loading.

The basic wing structure is a scaled up version of that of the Boeing 767 with extra gulling effect inboard to provide clearance for the engines. One of the ways the 777 wing differed from earlier Boeing wings was that more automation was used in the manufacture and assembly, which meant that more controls had to be in existence to monitor the spanwise and overall curvature of the aerofoil. Aluminium is used in all the primary structure, which consists of front and rear spars, upper and lower spar chords, webs, skin panels, stringers and ribs. The wing consists of three torsion-box assemblies built from the front and rear spars. In the outboard sections, the ribs are perpendicular to the rear spar, and spanwise beams provide support in the centre-section box. The outboard wings are joined to the centre-section at the fuselage side root-rib, and machined skin panels are joined by splice plates. A new Alcoa-developed aluminium alloy, 7155T77, has been used for the upper wing skin, which had improved compression load capability. The upper wing stringers are made from extrusions of the same material, to stiffen the skin panels integrally. The lower wing skins use a 2,000 series aluminium alloy, which is better suited

to the higher tension loads experienced. Total fuel capacity of the standard 777 wing, both the outer sections, and the centre-section, is 25,806UK gal (117,300 litres), and traditional baffle ribs contain the fuel in various compartments to avoid it sloshing around.

The secondary wing structure supports the skins, fairings and control surface mechanisms. The leading edge slats have a simple outboard operation, similar to the older Boeing 727 tri-jet, while the inboard units are operated by complicated linkage and ball-screw drives to obtain the necessary operating geometry. On the inboard trailing edge are double-slotted flaps, with single-slotted units just outboard. An inboard high-speed aileron also acts as a slotted flap during take-off and landing, and traditional ailerons are outboard, with assistance from spoilers on the top wing surface. The spoilers also act as speed brakes, and lift-dump on landing.

Following the requirement from American Airlines that the 777 be compatible with their airport gates, Boeing designed the outer 21ft 3in (6.5m) of the wing-tip, to be folding vertically upwards – somewhat like naval aircraft. The system was only designed to operate when the aircraft was on the ground, and travelling at less than 50kts (90km/h). The hingeline for the folding section is at about 80 percent span, inboard of the aileron and two sections of leading edge slats, and hydraulic latch pins would ensure locking down of the wingtip during flight. There is no fuel in the moving wingtip, but to date, no airline has specified this folding feature.

UNDERCARRIAGE
On the undercarriage, each of the main legs carries a six-wheel bogie, with three pairs in tandem, giving a similar pavement

loading to the DC-10, but without the need for the extra centre-fuselage unit. The aft axle of the main gear has up to eight degrees of steering movement to assist the nosewheel steering, reducing the turn radius and tyre wear by scrubbing. The brakes are controlled by a digital auto-brake and anti-skid system, with individual brake temperatures indicated on the cockpit displays. The main gear structure is manufactured from titanium to save weight, and it is supported from the rear wing spar and an additional rear beam. A hydraulic actuator positions the main bogies at a 13 degree nose-up position for take-off and landing, and sets it at a five degree nose-down position for retraction. The nose gear resembles a scaled-up version of those used in the Boeing 757 and 767. Indicator lights tell the tug driver whether the brakes are off (a blue light), with amber for parking brake and red for brakes on.

TAIL ASSEMBLY

The major area in which composites are used by Boeing in a primary structure for the first time is the tail assembly. The main assembly box of the fin is a carbonfibre-reinforced structure, consisting of front and rear spars, as well as the ribs. The fin skin panels are also made from carbonfibre composites. Out of the three fin spars, the main and front spars are built from carbonfibre-reinforced plastic, only the rear auxiliary spar being made from aluminium. The rudder consists of a pair of spars, plus ribs, all made from carbonfibre, covered by carbonfibre epoxy sandwich skins. The small dorsal fin is made-up from aluminium frames and skins. The horizontal tailplane is made in two parts, mated directly together in the relatively empty tail fuselage section, with a dihedral forming a shallow V. By joining the two parts directly, instead of using a traditional tailplane centre-section, there was some 50 percent reduction of parts, making it cheaper to build. The construction of the tailplane and elevators is similar to the fin and rudder, with the minimum use of metal fittings. The distinctive vertical-blade tailcone helps to reduce induced drag by smoothing the stagnant flow which had been detected around the conical tailcone of the 767.

ELECTRICS

The systems' architecture for the 777 was generally similar to the 767, or any other twin-jet airliner, despite the service-ready concepts, including ETOPS in time for the original first airline delivery. The only major change added to help with the early ETOPS was an extra air-starter, in addition to the normal electrical starter, for the

TOP: Composites were used for the first time in primary structures with the fin, tailplane, rudder and elevators. This produces a light structure which is not prone to corrosion. *Philip Birtles*

ABOVE: The Allied Signal 331-500 APU is located in the tail-cone with the exhaust out of the port side. The APU has proved to be exceptionally reliable from the initial entry into service, and is essential for starting the engines at the less well equipped airfields. *Philip Birtles*

LEFT: JAL 'Starjet' 777-246 JA8981 WA023 *Sirius* after departure, with take-off flaps, and showing clearly the six-wheel main undercarriage units. *JAL*

APU. There needed to be a confidence in excess of 99 percent of the APU starting in the air, after a cold soak at altitude, when an ETOPS diversion was required because of an engine shut-down. It was also logical to use existing systems proven in an ETOPS environment, rather than attempt a new design, which would have to be proved in service all over again. The airline customers requested greater functional control over all the systems, which meant digital electronics throughout, using an ARINC 629 multiplex digital database. This allows precise control over the lighting and cabin temperature, providing greater systems' redundancy for improved despatch reliability.

Quite naturally the 777 uses a great deal of electrical power, as it is vital to the majority of the aircraft systems. As an example, the standard electronics bay in previous Boeing airliners could provide up to 14kVa, while the in-flight passenger entertainment system alone requires up to 22kVa in the 777. The largest power requirement is the ovens, but Boeing's first use of fly-by-wire control inputs underlines the need for a multi-redundant power system.

The primary electrical generating system consists of three 120kVa Sundstrand constant-speed integrated-drive generators. Two are driven by the aircraft engines and the third by the APU. Two generators are capable of providing the normal power for the aircraft systems, but if one fails, perhaps due to an engine shut down, an automatic load-shedding system begins to reduce the power requirements of the galleys, without affecting the needs of the flightdeck, or passenger cabin. A second shaft on each engine generates a further 20kVa to power the flight control system. In an extreme emergency, when all other power has failed, a wind-driven drop-out ram-air turbine is housed in the wing-root fairing. Previous ram-air turbines were only capable of developing hydraulic power, with batteries providing the emergency electrics, for continued control of the aircraft in the descent, but the unit fitted to the 777 also generates up to 7.5kVa, since there is a greater reliance on electrical control than hydraulics on the 777.

In switching to electrical fly-by-wire controls, Boeing made one of the biggest changes by using a drive architecture similar to that used in flight simulators, connected to the traditional control column, since their operations are largely electrically driven. The major change from the simulator layout was to space them further apart, to avoid simultaneous damage from a bird strike. The analogue movement of the controls by the pilot is transferred electrically to a unit known as actuator control electronics (ACE). These are just analogue to digital devices, without any software, to convert the input to the actuator to move the control surfaces as required. Because the 777 is an unstable, relaxed-pitch-mode aircraft, a pitch rate sensor has been installed to assist in the control of the aircraft.

STATE OF THE ART TECHNOLOGY

The pilot's control inputs pass to three primary flight-control (PFC) computers. These GEC-Marconi produced PFCs use flight-control laws developed by Boeing to protect the integrity of the aircraft, but ensure that the pilot can over-ride them and maintain ultimate control. The flight-control laws of the Boeing

ABOVE: Because the 777 uses more electrical power than any of Boeing's previous designs, the emergency drop-down ram-air turbine can generate an improved 7.5kVa as well as hydraulic power. It is located in the trailing edge of the wing-root fairing, and this one has tape around it to bring attention, avoiding damage from passing vehicles. *Philip Birtles*

RIGHT AND FOLLOWING PAGES: A typical turn-round of JAL 777-246 JA8984 WA068 at Tokyo Haneda Airport, showing the access doors for cargo, catering and servicing.

ABOVE RIGHT: Unloading cargo from the forward hold.

BELOW RIGHT: Opening up the rear cargo doors after arrival, for unloading to commence.
Martin Prozesky photos with permission from JAL

777 are governed by speed stability, which means that when the control column is displaced, it will return to its previous position, giving the pilot an indication of where the aircraft is going. The 777 is therefore trimmed to a set speed, and any changes from this speed will cause the pitch to change.

The 777 is Boeing's first truly digital aircraft, with more than 2.6 million lines of software code incorporated in the avionics and cabin entertainment system, compared to only 400,000 lines in the Boeing 747-400. Out of the total, around 600,000 lines are dedicated to the Honeywell-produced Aircraft Information Management System (AIMS), which displays information on communications, flight and thrust management, central maintenance, condition monitoring, data conversion, engine operating data and flight data acquisition all into one unit. Two AIMSs are installed, each one of which can operate the aircraft.

ABOVE: Unloading cargo containers from the rear main hold. Loose items can also be stowed in the smaller extreme rear hold.

RIGHT: Refuelling at the underwing pressure pick-up point, with jet fuel being supplied from underground tanks.

LEFT: Flight catering is supplied through both the forward and rear service doors for the galleys. Adequate clearance has to be available around the aircraft for all the turnaround functions to be completed without any confliction.
Martin Prozesky photos with permission from JAL

ABOVE: The tow-bar is located on the front of the nose-wheel leg ready for push-back.

ABOVE RIGHT: With the finger docks pulled back after the passengers have boarded, the 777 is made ready for push-back.

MAIN PICTURE: Push-back continues, with two ground engineers in attendance to unhitch the tow-bar.
Martin Prozesky photos with permission from JAL

The Honeywell air-data inertial-reference system is a key part of the aircraft avionics systems. This fault-tolerant, skewed axis laser-gyro inertial unit provides inertial information and air data to such a high level of redundancy, that the airline may not even be aware that there is a failure. A secondary attitude air-data reference unit provides a back-up data source.

To maintain a high despatch reliability, and sometimes to comply with ETOPS, the pneumatic systems need to have a high level of integrity. Heat-exchangers have been added to the air-conditioning packs, to achieve full cooling, even with one pack failed.

FUEL AND HYDRAULIC SYSTEMS

The architecture of the hydraulic system is based on the one used for the 767, with three independent systems giving the capability of a safe landing on only one system. Each of the systems is powered by engine-driven pumps, generators and bleed air in combination to minimise the effect of power-source failures in the hydraulic system.

Apart from eliminating the outboard-wing surge-tanks, the fuel system is almost identical to the 767, the highly efficient wing taking the aircraft up to 9,600nm (17,800km), with full wing tanks, without having to put fuel in the area of the optional wing fold.

AIRPLANE OF THE FUTURE

In terms of overall size, the Boeing 777 is initially between the 747-400 and the smaller 767, the aircraft being conceived as a trans-continental replacement for the tri-jet McDonnell Douglas DC-10 and the Lockheed Tristar. It has, however, been developed into a multi-role airliner, creating major competition for the Airbus A340 and the McDonnell Douglas MD-11 over the longest international routes. By arriving later in the market place than the competition, the 777 was able to avoid the worst of the early 1990s' economic slump, and was tailored more to the long-range requirements of the prospective customers.

As part of the family development, the Boeing 777 is expected to lead the 400-seat long-range jet airliner market, with predicted sales up to 2010 expected to be worth in the region of $300 billion. This value is about 40 percent of the total market, predicted to be worth $780 billion. The major competition will be from the Airbus family, as McDonnell Douglas has cancelled development of the MD-11 series, and is merging with Boeing.

The initial A-market aircraft are now on order and entering service to replace the TriStars and DC-10s on medium-range and US domestic routes. The heaviest of these A-market aircraft, with a maximum take-off weight of 534,600lb (243,000kg), can fly 305 passengers up to 4,820nm (8,900km). The later, longer-range B-market 777s, as ordered by BA, will bring the economies of the Boeing 747-200 with better ranges than the 747-400, complementing the lower capacity 767-300ERs.

Long-term plans are to develop the ultra long-range C-market version, and the high capacity 777 Stretch, the latter always being allowed for in the future plans, with even the existing undercarriage being sized to cope with the extra rotation clear-ance required on take-off with the longer fuselage. The 777 Stretch will be 32ft 10in (10m) longer, at 242ft 9in (74m), which will be some 11ft 6in (3.5m) longer than the existing 747, and it will accommodate up to 550 passengers in a high-density layout, or 420 in a mixed class, making it a good replacement for the early 747s.

Boeing, therefore has a strong family of jet airliners for the foreseeable future, capable of competing in the world markets, the only missing type at the moment being the ultra-large transport, which might eventually carry up to 1,000 passengers, and against which Airbus also expects to provide competition.

VARIANTS

The Boeing 777 was always planned to be capable of development into a family of airliners, covering a wide capability of range and payloads, and keeping the type competitive well into the 21st century. The initial aircraft was a little short on range, which was rapidly corrected by adding fuel and some strengthened structure to become what was originally known as the B-market aircraft, and was later known as the -200IGW, signifying increased gross weight. Essential to all the developments is the capability of the engine manufacturers to produce more power, with as few changes as possible, to keep costs down.

The stretched version of the aircraft was being studied in mid-1992 with a planned in-service date of 1998. The objective was to carry a further 60 passengers over the same range as the initial model with a 19-frame stretch adding about 33ft 3in (10.14m) to the basic model, allowing an additional pallet in the forward cargo bay. Cathay was on early supporter of the stretched version with an increased gross weight of almost 22,000lb (10,000kg) and a longer range of about 5,000nm (8,050km) The stretched version, which would be about 242ft 9in (74m) long. was expected to carry up to 420 passengers and 44 LD-3 cargo containers, making the aircraft 33 percent more efficient than the 747-100. To power this version, the Rolls-Royce Trent engines would need to develop up to 89,000lb (396kN) thrust. By the second quarter of 1993 Boeing had approved the stretched 777 in principle, but were seeking launch customers for around 20 aircraft, which included not only Cathay, but also other Asian operators, such as ANA, JAS and Thai.

In addition to the stretched versions, Boeing was also looking at increasing the range of the standard version by taking advantage of the increase in power of the engines. A heavier long-range version of the basic IGW B-market aircraft could have its take-off weight increased to 287.16ton (291,755kg) from the standard 268ton (272,288kg), giving an increase in range from 6,345nm (11,750km) to 7,300nm (13,500km). Singapore Airlines were a target customer for this version.

In early 1995, Pratt & Whitney announced the launch of the PW4098 version of the PW4000 series of fan engines, developing 98,000lb (436kN) thrust for the heavier versions of the 777, up to a gross take-off weight of 660,000lb (299,640kg). The extra power would increase the range with 305 passengers, from 7,400nm (13,650km) to around 7,695nm (14,250km). The extra power would also allow the stretched version to carry 450

passengers up to 5,508nm (10,200km). Certification of the new version of the engine was planned for September 1997.

As another part of the family, Boeing was studying a short-bodied, ultra-long-range version of the 777 in the first half of 1995, known as the 777-100X. The reduction in length of between nine and 14 frames would allow the aircraft to carry 250 passengers up to 9,000nm (16,650km), the major interest coming from American Airlines, but with potential from SIA, Qantas and Cathay. Destinations which could be served by this version included Dallas–Tokyo and Hong Kong–New York. The maximum take-off weight was close to the 631,730lb (287,150kg) upper limit being defined for the IGW version, avoiding any additional structural strengthening, although as it would follow about a year after the 777-300X, it could be fitted with the structurally reinforced wing. Power would come from the same engine developments with 90,000lb (400kN) thrust being developed for the IGW market.

By mid-1995, Cathay was pressing for the stretched version of the 777, and was planning on using the balance of seven of the initial order to acquire this version, without converting any of the 11 options. Cathay required this high density version for short-range regional routes. Meanwhile Rolls-Royce had already defined thrust levels of up to 95,000lb (423kN) for the Trent developments to provide power for the heavier weight 777s. The Trent 895 was targeted for certification in September 1997. The basic engine was expected to be capable of developing 100,000lb (444kN) of thrust without increasing the fan diameter, and the basic core was capable of 102,000lb (453kN). During testing, the development engines had reached more than 106,100lb (471kN).

As the Paris Show approached, there was speculation of the imminent launch of the 777-300 by Boeing at the show, backed by orders for around 30 aircraft from ANA, Cathay, Egyptair,

ABOVE: The first modest development of the 777 over the initial production aircraft was the IGW version of the Series 200. The 777-200 IGW has the same overall dimensions as the initial aircraft, but carries an additional 14,220gal (53,826 litres) of fuel in the wing centre-section. With the take-off weight increased from 545,000lb (247,210kg) to 632,500lb (286,900kg), the IGW version can fly 7,150nm (13,230km) compared with 5,150 nm (9,525 km) of the early 777, opening up new routes, such as London–Los Angeles, Chicago–Seoul and San Francisco–Tokyo. This aircraft, N782UA WA057, first flew 14 February 1997 and was the 50th 777 to be delivered. It departed Everett on 7 March to become the 17th 777 to join the United fleet, and the first 777 IGW. *Boeing*

KAL and Thai. The Asian carriers needed a high-density medium-range aircraft for their regional routes, as well as being required in Japan to replace the well-worn 747s used on domestic routes. By this time the stretch was expected to add 10 frames, or 17ft 5in (5.3m) forward of the wing, and nine frames or 15ft 9in (4.8m) aft. In the Japanese high density version, up to 550 passengers could be carried.

In the event Boeing did confirm the go-ahead of the 777-300 at the Paris Show in June 1995, with orders totalling 31 aircraft from ANA, Cathay, KAL and Thai. These orders consisted of 20 new sales, and the conversion of 11 existing orders. ANA placed the largest commitment – for 10 777-300s with options on five more, the first aircraft to enter service in mid-1998. Thai ordered six of the stretched version, with deliveries commencing in September 1998, and KAL increased its order to 12 aircraft by adding four new 777-300s. As expected, Cathay changed seven of its existing order to the -300, the first to take delivery to be in May 1998. ANA and KAL aircraft will be powered by the P&W PW4098; Cathay and Thai are planning to use the Trent developments. Take-off weight was set at 572,000lb (260,000kg) with the 84,375lb (375kN) engines, but the structure allowed the maximum take-off weight to reach 660,000lb (300,000kg).

By the middle of 1995, Boeing was expecting to launch the 777-100X within 15 months, for service entry in 1999. To take

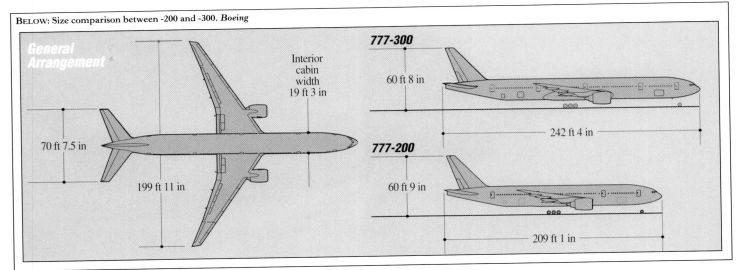

BELOW: Size comparison between -200 and -300. *Boeing*

General Arrangement

Interior cabin width 19 ft 3 in

70 ft 7.5 in

199 ft 11 in

777-300

60 ft 8 in

242 ft 4 in

777-200

60 ft 9 in

209 ft 1 in

the most advantage of the ultra-long-range, air rights in the Asia/Pacific region would need to be liberalised, including the negotiation of new bilateral and overflight agreements, factors largely out of the control of Boeing. The estimated maximum range was expected to be in the region of 8,600nm (16,000km), which was further than any existing airliner, including the 747-400, and would be able to open up new destination pairs.

In response to the interest by Taiwanese carriers China Airlines (CAL) and EVA Air in a 777 combi, Boeing stated in August 1995, that they could have this type available for delivery in 1997. The proposed combi aircraft would have accommodation for up to 220 passengers, and a maximum of seven cargo pallets on the main deck, weighing up to a total of 83,6000lb (38,000kg). Boeing had to decide whether to manufacture the combi directly on the existing production line, or complete the aircraft as standard 777-200s, followed by conversion. However by mid-1997, neither airline had confirmed their interest in the 777, and no doubt the LoIs had elapsed.

By December 1995 Boeing was well advanced with the detail planning of the design for the 777-300, and expected to be complete by February. Half the design was released for manufacture by September 1996, and major assembly was planned to start in March 1997. The changes were kept to a simple minimum, the object being to fly more people further, and although Boeing was in the midst of a manual workers' strike, the first flight was planned for October 1997, with first delivery to Cathay in May 1998. In order to keep costs down, Boeing reduced the development costs by 30 percent from the 777-200, cutting the development timescale from 42 months to 32 months from firm configuration to delivery. Only around 15 percent of the parts are unique, and the production cycle was shortened by 25 percent.

Ground manoeuvring cameras were fitted, because the turning radius being greater than the Boeing 747. Other changes included a tail-skid to protect the longer rear fuselage during rotation at take-off, and a fifth A-type emergency exit door was fitted on each side of the revised centre-fuselage to allow up to 550 passengers to be carried, although most airlines were expected to select three-class layouts of between 368 and 394 passengers.

By February 1996 Boeing was also looking at an ultra-long-range version of the 777-200, as an alternative to the short fuselage 777-100X, since the demand from the airlines appeared to require the long range of the -100X with the capacity of the 777-200. By going this route, Boeing would be able to have the ultra-long-range version available a year earlier, and therefore be more competitive. Additional fuel could be located in the outer wings, tail and increased in the centre-section, taking total fuel capacity to 29,920lb (13,600kg), and the maximum take-off weight to 313ton (318,000kg). Power would have to come from the 95,000–98,000lb (425–435kN) thrust engines, which were already being developed for the 777-300. Studies continued during 1996, with September targeted as the decision date between the -100X and the improved -200X, to allow detailed design work to commence. Depending upon which option was chosen, the development time would be between three and five years, but the decision was to be market-driven, and could result in both versions going into development. The advantage of the -200X is that it would offer 8–9 percent lower seat per km costs than the smaller capacity -100X, but the aircraft would not be available until 2001, two years after the -100X, due to the extra time needed to certificate the more powerful engines for first the -300, and then the -200X. The -100X, however, would be fitted with the existing 90,000lb (400kN) engines, due to enter service in 1997.

General Electric had originally planned an intermediate development of the GE90 to a power of between 423 and 436kN, followed later by a much more powerful version capable of thrust levels of between 95,175lb (467kN) and 115,200lb (512kN). However at the end of April 1996, the new growth plan was expected to produce thrust levels up to 100,000lb (445kN) by 1999, by-passing the staged growth of rivals Pratt & Whitney and Rolls-Royce.

Due to changes in the competitive environment, Boeing was unable to make the decision to launch the new long-range derivative of the 777 by the planned September 1996. New types were on offer by Airbus and McDonnell Douglas, which gave the airlines greater choice, the two major 777 prospects being divided on their selection. American Airlines favoured the larger -200X, while Singapore preferred the shorter -100X, and the two versions were really aimed at two different market slots.

Meanwhile Boeing was also studying a heavier 777-300 with a maximum take-off weight of around 688,600lb (313,000kg), although the existing structure was only strong enough for take-off weights of up to 660,000lb (300,000kg). By November Boeing was considering an even longer-range version of the -200X, with a strengthened wing, increased fuel capacity and a new wingtip, but the airlines had yet to decide what they would require. The maximum take-off weight had increased to 709,148lb (322,340kg), and extra fuel would be in the outer wing, reserved for folding but not adopted by any airline. In service date had slipped to 2000, but there was no sense of urgency from the airlines, who wanted to assess the likely growth of the ultra-long-range less dense routes.

In November, with relatively few engines in service on the 777, General Electric put on hold plans to develop the 100,000lb (445kN) thrust GE90-100B fan engine.

With the sale of 777s to Air France, Boeing considered an interim increase in the maximum take-off weight for service entry from 1998 onwards. With the weight increased to 646,800lb (294,000kg), from 660,000lb (287,000kg), the range would be up to 7,500nm (13,875km). To cope with the increased loads, the aircraft could be fitted with the reinforced

landing gear designed for the -300, and the wing skins would be thickened, adding 500lb (227kg) to the empty weight. The 44,914US gal (170,000) litre fuel capacity would be unchanged, but the higher all-up weight would allow the aircraft to carry more fuel with a full load of 305 passengers. Performance penalties would include a 950ft (290m) longer take-off field length, a lower initial cruise altitude of 34,000ft (10,350m), a lower engine-out altitude of 12,250ft (3,736m) and a one-per-cent rise in fuel consumption per seat.

In early 1997, Boeing were tending towards the longer range -200X, rather than the smaller -100X, and were planning on a launch alongside the -300X in June. The -200X maximum take-off weight would be in the range of 700,000–730,000lb (318,000–331,500kg), depending upon range requirements. The 250-seat aircraft would be able to operate over ranges of 8,500–9,000nm (15,725–16,650km), depending on the MTOW. Additional fuel could be carried in the outer wing and horizontal stabiliser. Operators showing the greatest interest in this new version were American, SIA and MSA for the long thin Pacific routes from Asia to the US West Coast. Meanwhile United and JAL were prime candidates for the 6,993nm (12,950km) range 777-300X.

The Boeing Board finally approved the 777-200X and -300X specifications in February 1997, to allow them to be offered to prospective airlines, with a planned launch at the Paris Show in June. Boeing claimed the 777-200X would be the world's longest-range airliner, capable of carrying 298 passengers in a three-class layout up to 8,600nm (15,900km). Meanwhile the

BELOW: High above the clouds, Emirates first of seven 777-21Hs, A6-EMD WA030, makes its maiden flight from Paine Field, Everett on 2 March 1996; it was delivered to the airline on 2 March. *Emirates*

-300X will be able to carry 355 passengers up to 6,589nm (12,200km). Detail design of both variants is planned to be complete by May 1998, with the prospective airlines being involved in the working group from May 1997. Certification is planned for the -200X in August 2000, with service entry the following month, and the -300X will be ready for service in January 2001.

To simplify production and reduce engineering costs, the two versions will be identical apart from the fuselage plugs, 17ft 6in (5.34m) ahead of the wing, and 15ft 9in (4.80m) behind the leading edge. The wing, fuselage, tailplane and fin will all be strengthened, and a new wingtip will increase span by 2ft 3in (0.69m) on either side. Fuel will be carried in the new extended wing, but instead of using the tailplane as an additional fuel tank, optional palletised auxiliary fuel tanks will be offered, to be installed in the rear cargo hold of the -200X.

Power will come from the 102,000lb (454kN) thrust engines being developed by all three engine manufacturers, which should be achieved by development of the existing engines, without an expensive increase in fan size. GE was expected to offer the 102,150lb (454kN) GE90-102B, Pratt & Whitney the 98,1000lb (436kN) PW4098, and Rolls-Royce, the Trent 8100, which although initially rated at 98,325lb (437kN), gives the same performance as the rival 100,125lb (445kN) engines. Only two weeks after the board approval, GE became the first engine company to sign a formal agreement with Boeing for the higher thrust engine to power the new developments. The MOU was reported to cover the development of the 100,125lb (445kN) GE90-102B for deliveries commencing in September 2000, to be followed by the higher thrust 102,600lb (456kN) GE90-102B to be available from mid-2002. Three of the potential launch customers for the -200X already had ordered Trent-powered 777s, putting pressure on Rolls-Royce to commit to the more powerful engine, who were studying the Trent 8102 developing up to 100,125lb (445kN) of thrust. Korean Air was already a user of P&W engines, who at that time were not committed to more than 98,000lb (436kN) of thrust, but the airline were a prospect for the new developments. Rolls-Royce reached an agreement with Boeing at the end of April for the development of the planned 100,000lb (444kN) Trent 8100 engine. In fact there was also agreement that the development should be advanced by nine months to allow certification and service entry by 2001.

The engine manufacturers are therefore critical to the progressive development of the Boeing 777, but the high cost of the engine development has to be weighed against the risk of obtaining enough airline customers to make a reasonable return on the enormous investment involved, especially with the keen competition between the engine manufacturers.

RIGHT: The major development of the 777 is the stretched 777-300 which will be capable of carrying 20 percent more passengers than the -200 and serving as a replacement for the early 747s. The 33ft (10m) increase in length of the fuselage will allow a typical three-class layout to increase the passenger capacity from 305 to 368 passengers, or up to 550 passengers in an all-economy layout. With a maiden flight in 1997, initial deliveries are planned for early 1998 to Cathay Pacific. *Boeing*

5 IN SERVICE

ORDERS

The launch order for the Boeing 777 came from United Airlines on 15 October 1990. It was in two parts: a firm commitment for 34 aircraft and an option on a further 34. The 777 order was included on a massive United shopping list for various Boeing aircraft — including 60 Boeing 747-400s! — the most valuable order for commercial aircraft to that date, worth some $22 billion. The United commitment allowed Boeing formally to start the 777 programme on 29 October 1990. The engine order — worth about $4 billion — was won by Pratt & Whitney with the PW4073. In its initial form the engine was expected to develop 73,000lb (328.5kN) of thrust.

The United requirement was for the intercontinental B-market aircraft, seating up to 363 passengers in a two-class layout, with a range of 4,200nm (7,700km) and a maximum take-off weight of 514,800lb (234,000kg). All Nippon Airways (ANA) had been keen to take advantage of sharing the launch customer benefits, but as it was still evaluating the competing Airbus A330/340 and the McDonnell Douglas MD-11, the airline did not place the order until the end of November. Following the completion of the evaluations, ANA ordered 15 A-market 777s, with options on a further 10; they would work on high-density Japanese domestic operations and had to seat up to 400 passengers. In ANA operations, ETOPS was not a requirement, and the airline also selected the PW4073 as the powerplant in October 1991.

The launch customer for the B-market 777 came with an order for two aircraft from the French independent airline Eurolair in June 1991: in the event this order was never confirmed, and later lapsed. At the Paris Air Show in the same month, Thai Airways International announced firm orders for six regional A-market 777s worth $900 million, with options on a further six aircraft, the contract being subject to the Thai government approval.

A major political and industrial storm raged in Europe when British Airways placed its order for the 777 on 21 August 1991. Not only were there objections from Airbus Industrie in Europe, but the choice of General Electric GE90 engines, instead of the traditional Rolls-Royce engines, caused serious concern in Britain, particularly as other airlines would normally have expected BA to have ordered the British engines, and it was believed that the sales prospects for the Trent engine would

RIGHT: United Airlines was the launch customer for the Boeing 777, with its 15 October 1990 order for 34 firm commitments and 34 options, all powered by Pratt & Whitney PW4073 engines. Because of the cost of mounting air-to-air photo sessions, Boeing tends to leave this to their customers, but an exception was made when 777-222 WA002 N774UA was photographed near Seattle during the flight development programme. This aircraft made its first flight on 15 July 1994 and, after refurbishment from the flight test programme, was delivered to United on 29 March 1996. *Boeing*

TOP: The first 777 to be delivered, N777UA WA007 was handed over to United on 17 May 1995 outside the Seattle Museum of Flight. To open the handover ceremony, WA001 flew by in an aerial salute. *Boeing*

ABOVE: The first Boeing 777 for ANA, JA8197 was handed over at Seattle during a celebration of the Tanabata Star Festival, and was delivered on 31 October 1995. At this ceremony, the aircraft carried the ANA rather than the more usual 777 logo on the fin. *Boeing*

suffer accordingly. Although not claimed to be part of the contract, General Electric also took over responsibility for the BA engine overhaul facility in Wales. This made sense for BA, since the company is not really in the specialised engine overhaul business. The GE90 engine order was worth some $1.4 billion, with engine certification due in November 1994 at a thrust of 87,400lb (388.8kN). The BA 777 order was worth overall $3.6 billion and was for 15 firm deliveries, with options on another 15 aircraft; the order also included commitments for further Boeing 747-400s. The BA deliveries were planned to commence in September 1995, with the first five to the A-market standard with ETOPS a firm requirement. The first aircraft were needed for BA routes to the Middle East, and to the US East Coast; the remainder of the fleet would be the long-range B-market 777 IGW configuration for BA's intercontinental routes. Deliveries were to be completed by 2002 with all the BA 777s having the same three-class seating layout carrying up to 313 passengers.

In September 1991, Nicki Lauda, the former racing driver and chairman of Austrian independent airline Lauda Air, ordered four 777s, worth $560 million. He wanted to replace

Lauda Air's 767s. Deliveries were scheduled for two aircraft in 1997 and the other two following in 2000, confirmation of the contract coming the next month.

The Asian region has been an important growth area for airlines, and therefore provided a good potential market for the high-density 777. Boeing salesmen turned potential into sales in November 1991 when Japan Airlines placed orders for 10 777s, with options for a further 10. The initial batch would be A-market models for Japanese domestic and regional use, but the possibility was left open that some of the options could be converted to the intercontinental B-market versions. The cabin was configured in a 380-passenger two-class layout, and deliveries were scheduled to commence from late 1995.

In mid-December 1991 Emirates, the Dubai-based airline, announced its intention to place an order worth $2 billion for seven 777s, with options on seven more. In the letter of intent to Boeing, Emirates stated its requirement for three A-models for delivery in 1996, the remainder of the firm order and options to be for the B-market version. Rolls-Royce won the engine order worth £200 million ($455 million) with the Trent 880 engine, which was expected to develop 80,000lb (363.6kN) of thrust in the improved 777A then on offer. It was also expected that when the 85,950lb (382kN) thrust Trent 844-powered 777Bs were delivered, the earlier A-series aircraft may be returned, unless they proved suitable for the shorter dense regional routes. The initial Emirates 777s were configured with a total of 375 seats, taking full advantage of the 10-abreast layout, and the order was finally confirmed in June 1992.

Despite the sales for the Boeing 777 in 1991, it was a bad year for all jet airliner orders, reaching only 36 percent of the 1990 levels, but Boeing claimed a respectable overall total of 76 777 orders, 27 having been placed in 1991. Nevertheless the difficulties of 1991 did not improve immediately in 1992: United slowed its fleet expansion by deferring 122 orders and options for a number of Boeing types. The first aircraft was still

to be delivered in May 1995, but only four more 777s were to be delivered in the first year, a reduction of six aircraft. While United's overall orders were unaffected, the deliveries were stretched out over a longer period.

In February 1992, the Thai Government confirmed the Thai Airways order, increasing the firm orders to eight for the airline with six on option. At the same time, the selection of the Rolls-Royce Trent 870 engine was confirmed, bringing to three the main engine suppliers to the commercial 777 programme. By mid-1992 Thai Airways was again evaluating the choice between the 777 and Airbus A330 for a requirement for a further seven aircraft due to be added to the fleet by the end of the decade. However, a 85 percent fall in profits for the last quarter of 1992 caused the airline to consider deferring current deliveries as a cost-cutting exercise

Another Asian airline, and one of the original eight airlines who helped to define the 777, became a new customer, when Cathay Pacific chose the Boeing aircraft over the Airbus A330-400X in April 1992, with first deliveries wanted in 1996. The major deciding factor for Cathay was the plan for Boeing to offer at a later date a stretched version of the 777. The Hong Kong-based airline placed orders and options for 22 aircraft, worth some $3.4 billion. Cathay has for many years been a loyal customer of Rolls-Royce, and selected Trent 800 turbofans to power the fleet. The 11 777s on firm order were for the A-model, with a range of 4,900nm (9,000km), and the airline expects to convert its 11 options to the 6,588nm (12,200km) range B-model. The proposed stretched version of the 777, due to be available from 1998, is expected to be able to carry 60

BELOW: **All Nippon Airways had hoped to take advantage of sharing in the launch of the 777, but did not place its initial order until November 1990. ANA made a firm order for 15 aircraft with options on a further 10. They were for use on Japanese domestic routes, and therefore did not require an ETOPS capability. Boeing 777-281 WA016 JA8197, powered by Pratt & Whitney PW4073 engines, was the first for ANA and made its maiden flight on 31 August 1995.** *Boeing*

ABOVE: Boeing 777-236 G-ZZZA powered by two GE90 engines showing the flexibility of the outer wings, which can be seen curved upwards during flight. This aircraft was delivered to BA on 21 May 1996 – before BA's new colour scheme but after being refurbished following its use in the flight testing programme.
British Airways

more passengers in a 9.6m longer fuselage, than the A-model, but with the same range. The larger capacity aircraft will be required to replace the Boeing 747-200s on the high-density Asian regional routes, and will operate alongside the complementary A-models. Before Boeing defined the stretched version, the likely customer airlines were again asked to participate in the definition of the aircraft to ensure that it would fit their needs, a further 18 frames being considered the likely stretch.

Despite the disappointment of not winning the BA order, this had obviously not harmed Rolls-Royce as badly as had been expected, as the company had won more 777 customers than either of the other engine suppliers. In the second half of 1994, Cathay was having discussions with Boeing over the possibility of increasing the gross weight of the early A-models, due for delivery in March 1996, to give the aircraft extra range. The Rolls-Royce Trent engines were already being certificated to a thrust of 90,000lb (400kN), allowing the gross weight to be increased from 534,600lb (243,000kg) to 563,200lb (256,000kg), which would allow the 777s to fly from Hong Kong to Sydney direct, fully loaded with 10 tons (10,160kg) of extra freight. So, all that was needed was for Boeing to complete the new structural design to cope with the additional weight.

In mid-1992 Richard Branson, the Chairman of Virgin Atlantic, announced that the airline was considering up to eight new 777s, but that talks were also in hand with Airbus over the possibility of A340s (which were, in fact, eventually selected). Towards the end of 1992 the International Lease Finance Corporation (ILFC) placed orders for 81 aircraft and 25 options with Airbus and Boeing, including six orders and two options for GE90-powered B-market aircraft. Soon after United confirmed further cuts in orders of Boeing airliners, but the 777 package was not included, and it was agreed that, out of the firm orders for 34 777s, four would be completed as the longer-range B-market aircraft, with two for delivery in 1998 and the other two the following year. Meanwhile, the original four A-market aircraft would be offered to other customers.

Also at the end of 1992, China Southern ordered six 380-seat two-class 777s valued at $800 million, taking firm orders to almost 120 aircraft and options on a further 100. Discussions continued in April 1993 with China Aviation Supplies for further orders for Boeing 767s and 777s, but in mid-1994 China declared it would not be ordering any further new jet airliners for about 18 months, the money saved being used to improve the civil aviation safety measures and infrastructure. China's airline industry had been growing at the phenomenal rate of 30 percent per year — something that had completely overwhelmed the air traffic control systems, and led to a number of accidents in 1992 and 1993, killing a total of nearly 400 people. By September 1995, it was believed that Air China was ready to order 10 777s in a mixture of A and B-market types, with deliveries commencing in 1997, but due to political problems between China and the USA no progress was made. The first sign of an improvement was in mid-1996, when China Southern began negotiations with ILFC for an additional three 777-200 IGWs to be used on its planned services to the USA, two of the original order being already in service on domestic routes. The existing 777s could be used to fly to the US West Coast, but would require a technical stop at Fairbanks in Alaska. Relations were showing signs of significant improvement between the USA and China in the spring of 1997, after a uccession of political and trade disputes, and it was hoped that Air China would be confirming its order for 10 777-200/300s with options on a further five, at the end of March. In fact on 4 March Air China placed an order for five 777-200s valued at about $685 million, with the expectation that a further order for five 777-200IGWs would be placed by the end of the year. Although no engine was selected at the time, the Pratt & Whitney PW4077 was expected to be the favourite as Air China's existing fleet is P&W-powered.

In spring 1993, with further drops in air passenger levels, Japan Air System decided to exchange six 747-400s on order, for seven 777s, part of an $869 million cost reduction programme. The first A-model 777 was scheduled for delivery in September 1996 and the decision was confirmed in mid-1993. It was also announced in July 1993 that the two Japanese rival airlines, ANA and JAL, were planning to set up a joint organisation to provide maintenance for the Boeing 777 fleets when they were delivered from 1995. To test the effectiveness of the idea, the agreement would initially cover spare parts supply and storage, and they were expecting to invite JAS to join the group. JAS selected the Pratt & Whitney PW4084 engines for its 777s in November 1993, following the selection of the same engine by ANA in October 1991, leaving JAL to decide by early 1994. With continuing economic difficulties, ANA undertook a fleet review at the end of 1994, which could have delayed deliveries of the 777s, the airline having experienced increased competition because of the deregulation of the Japanese airline industry.

However, the air transport industry gradually strengthened and Continental placed what was then considered to be a huge order for Boeing airliners in May 1993. The orders for 92 aircraft, with options on 98 more, included five firm orders for B-model 777s with options on five more, the engine choice being the GE90. On 10 June 1997 Continental signed a letter of intent with Boeing for an exclusive purchase of a further five Boeing 777-200s, as well as 30 of the new 767-400ERs; the 777s were to be delivered from September 1998.

Gulf Air signed a letter of intent in November 1993 for up to 12 777s — an order potentially worth $2 billion — powered by GE90 engines. The order was expected to consist of six B-market 777s, with deliveries commencing in 1998 and options on six more. The 777s would be in addition to the earlier delivered Airbus A340s, and would be operated from Bahrain to destinations in Asia, Australia and Europe. Unfortunately, as happens so often in the aviation industry, another order failed to materialise when, in April 1995, Gulf Air decided not to order 777s.

By the end of 1993, Saudia was beginning to look at fleet modernisation with the 777, A330/340 and MD-11 being considered as Boeing 747-100 and TriStar replacements. By

BELOW: Japanese Airlines placed an order for 10 777s, with options on a further 10, in November 1991 for use on Japanese domestic services. In common with ANA, P&W engines were selected. The first JAL 777-246 — JA8981— made its maiden flight from the seasonally snowy Paine Field at Everett on 26 January 1996, and was delivered on 15 February named *Sirius* as the first in the JAL Star Jet fleet of 777s. *Boeing*

ABOVE: ANA 777 JA8199 made its first flight from Everett on 2 May 1996, and was the third to be delivered to the airline on 23 May. *Boeing*

ABOVE LEFT: Singapore Airlines prides itself in having one of the youngest fleets of jet airliners in the world. It placed its first order for 777-200 IGWs in November 1995 after an intensive evaluation. It was for 28 aircraft, with a commitment to acquire the larger, extended-range version, when available. The engine choice was the Rolls-Royce Trent. The first 777-212, 9V-SQA made its maiden flight on 6 May 1997, and was delivered soon after to Singapore painted in the special 50th anniversary colours. *Boeing*

BELOW LEFT: The first 777-267 to enter service with Cathay Pacific Airways, VR-HNC made its maiden flight on 4 April 1996 and was delivered on 9 May, carrying the 50th anniversary markings of the airline on the nose. The aircraft was configured for 50 business class and 293 economy class seats. *Boeing*

mid-1994 Saudia favoured Boeing as the overall supplier for its fleet replacement, with included in the plans up to 12 777s, to be powered by Rolls-Royce engines. A year later Saudia were considering a $6 billion order for Boeing and McDonnell airliners, including between 20 and 23 777s, with the engine choice left open. The major delays were caused, surprisingly, by Saudi Arabian difficulties in financing the orders, because of a heavy commitment to the USA for defence equipment. Saudia eventually signed a contract for a fleet of Boeing and McDonnell airliners on 26 October 1995, including firm orders for 23 777 IGWs to be powered by the 90,000lb (400kN) increased growth version of the GE90 fan engines.

Also at the end of 1993, Korean Air signed an order for 16 Boeing 777s in Seoul on 14 December, with the option to switch to the stretched version when it was available. The order covered eight 777 B-market aircraft, with options on eight more, the airline planning to use them from Seoul to North American destinations such as New York and Chicago. In mid-1995 KAL selected the 90,000lb (400kN) thrust PW4090 fan-engines for their 777s, Pratt & Whitney already being major suppliers to the KAL fleet. As part of the deal, P&W gave KAL a 10-year fleet guarantee covering no engine shutdowns, and only 0.7 maintenance shop visits per 1,000 hours flown.

With potential orders for the 777-300 from Cathay and Korean, Boeing was keen to obtain a further commitment from ANA or JAL, to allow full launch of this variant. ANA, having completed its fleet review, confirmed its order for 10 stretched 777-300s in September 1995, giving Boeing the confidence to launch this variant, which was essential to the development of the overall family of the basic type. The new version is planned to replace the 747SRs on the high density domestic network from 1998, and would be configured to carry up to 480 passengers. In the following month JAL joined the 777-300 club, by ordering five of the stretched version, worth $800 million. With a maximum high-density capacity of up to 520 passengers, the new 777s are intended to replace the slightly larger, but less economic 747-100Bs on the Japanese domestic routes. In mid-1996 JAL confirmed that the new aircraft would be powered by the PW4090 engines, similar to the existing -200s.

Singapore Airlines (SIA) has always aimed to operate the youngest fleet of any major airline, with an average age of five years, and at the end of June 1994, SIA announced orders for 747s and A340s, with leases of 777s. Up to eight 777s were to be leased, powered by the GE90 engines. The total orders were expected to double the airline fleet by 2003, and the 777s were planned to start replacing the Airbus A310s from 1996. By placing this order at a time of continuing air transport depression, SIA were able to take advantage of bargain prices for its fleet expansion into the next century. In September 1995, SIA widened its evaluation of the Boeing 777, to include the longer range B-market and the stretched -300 variants. Up to a further 17 aircraft would be required, and Airbus were competing with the A330/340 series. The poor sales record of the initial A-model gave concern for its resale value, and therefore the B-model IGW and the stretched version combination were of greater interest. The shorter range 777-300 with 400 to 550 seats would be an excellent successor to the 747-200/300 on high density routes. The B-model with 305 seats was seen as a good A310 replacement, but its range of 6,000nm (11,040km)

ABOVE: Once the Rolls-Royce certification flying was completed on the Cathay Pacific 777-267 WA014, it was registered VR-HNA and became the third to be delivered to the airline, on 23 August 1996. *Rolls-Royce*

ABOVE LEFT: In the second half of 1995 Egyptair ordered three 777-2000 IGWs, the first 777-266 being delivered to Cairo in May 1997. *Boeing*

BELOW LEFT: In February 1992, the Thai Government confirmed the Thai Airways requirement for the Boeing 777, covering eight firm orders, six options, and the selection of the Rolls-Royce Trent engines. Their first 777-2D7, WA025 HS-TJA, made its maiden flight from Paine Field, Everett on 1 March 1996. Named after the Thai province Lamphun, the 358-seat twin-jet was delivered on 31 March for service entry on routes from Bangkok to Hong Kong and Seoul. *Boeing*

was greater than that required for the SIA regional flights. Towards the end of 1995, SIA was having discussions with Boeing on what was becoming known as the extra long-range 777-100X. These discussions were including at least a dozen potential customers for this variant, and started with a brain-storming in Seattle in October. The proposed 777-100X was planned to be shorter than the -200, with a capacity for carry-ing up to 250 passengers in a three-class layout over ranges of 8,000nm (14,800km). The 777-100X would give SIA the capa-bility of flying from Singapore to the US West Coast direct. The airline need for a new aircraft had broadened from a regional A.310 replacement, to a very long range intercontinen-tal airliner. SIA finally made their decision in November 1995, electing to order 28 of the heavier 777-200 IGW version, with a commitment to acquire further larger and extended range 777s, as they become available. At the same time the Rolls-Royce Trent engines were selected, after an intense sales battle, which practically doubled the Trent orders for the 777 in one go. Singapore Aircraft Leasing, in which SIA has a 50 percent

share, also had six 777-200IGWs on order, with 10 more options, but the engine selection had not been made. In early 1997 SIA firmed up on two of the options, increasing the total number of 777s on order for the airline to 30 aircraft, with options remaining on a further 31. SIA also began to consider the ultra long-range 777-200X in competition with the Airbus A340-500 for direct flights from Singapore to the USA, the object to increase existing frequencies, as well as opening up new destinations.

In September of 1994, Air India was considering the acquisi-tion of a number of medium capacity long-range airliners as part of its fleet renewal plans. In this $4 billion plan, Air India were evaluating up to 13 Boeing 777s, Airbus A340s or McDonnell Douglas MD-11s.

During 1993, the first 777 sale was made in South America, with an order for three A-model aircraft from Transbrasil, powered by Rolls-Royce Trent engines. Deliveries were sched-uled to commence in 1996, but at the end of 1994, Transbrasil delayed delivery of the first aircraft until June 1997. The airline then decided to cancel its order for 777s in June 1995. 1994 had been a bad year for jet airliner sales, with no orders placed at all for the Boeing 777, and as a major cost-cutting exercise, Boeing had considered closing the narrow-body production lines at Renton, moving the 757 to Everett, and the 737 to Wichita.

KLM Royal Dutch Airlines began studying a major re-organisation plan in mid-1995, to replace the Boeing 747-300 fleet and planned MD-11 fleet with stretched 777-300s by 2000, for its long range routes. By the second half of 1995, air-liner orders were beginning to increase, with an order for three 777-200IGWs from Egyptair. However, due to the poor orders

for the previous years, deliveries fell for the fourth consecutive year. The first of the $400 million Egyptair order for 777s was scheduled for 1997, and the airline had chosen a three-class 308 passenger cabin layout.

In early 1995 China Airlines (CAL) signed a letter of intent (LoI) for four 777s during the Taiwanese Presidents visit to the USA. EVA, also of Taiwan, followed with a letter of intent for four, as yet unlaunched, combi versions of the 777, with seating for up to 220 passengers, and up to 83,600lb (38,000kg) of cargo on seven pallets on the main deck. Both these LoIs were not binding, but just declared an interest.

Following a highly competitive three-sided battle between Boeing, Airbus and McDonnell Douglas, Boeing was success-ful in winning an order from South African Airways (SAA) in November 1995. The order was for seven 777-200s, as well as

two additional 747-400s, the total being worth $960 million but the engine choice remained. The 777s would allow SAA to expand their frequencies to Asia and the Middle East operating with the older 747s. A major condition with th contract, was for Boeing to offer up to 80 percent of the valu of the order in offset contracts to South Africa. These discus sions continued for more than six months from the origina order, which delayed the selection of the engine and put bac the delivery of the airliners to SAA. After a further thre months without a firm decision on offsets, the SAA order wa put on hold, while the airline decided whether to reduce th number of aircraft, or considered acquiring them by lease, th engine decision still having not been made. Discussions wer reported to be restarted in early 1997 while SAA were als undergoing a major management reorganisation, the possibl

LEFT: Having been one of the original group of airlines who helped define the 777, Cathay Pacific placed their order in April 1992 for a total of 22 aircraft, including options, and selected the Rolls-Royce Trent engine. The firm orders covered 11 aircraft, and as launch customer for the Trent engines, the first aircraft, N77772 WA014, which made its maiden flight on 26 May 1995, participated in the certification programme for the airframe/engine combination, Boeing

powered 777s, included five of the stretched -300, which were selected to increase frequencies, and open up new thinner routes to the Middle East, South Africa and South America. Included in the deal were options on two further 777s, with an intent to acquire a further 35 aircraft to be selected as required, and available, from the future 777-100X and any larger 747 developments. ILFC further added to its fleet of aircraft available for lease in March 1996, by ordering a range of Boeing and Airbus airliners, including 18 777-200s/-300s, plus two options. Ten of the 777s would be powered by the GE90 engines, five by the PW4000 and Rolls-Royce Trent 800 for the remaining three aircraft. Deliveries of the 777 were scheduled between 1999 and 2004.

By 1996, the travel boom had begun to return to the airlines, and the cut-backs of three years prior had changed into a need for more capacity in the future. One of the airlines experiencing the improved economy was United, the 777 launch customer, who were negotiating with Boeing in May for up to 35 longer range aircraft worth about $3 billion, and including 15 or 17 777s. The majority of these would be for the stretched 777-300, as were also some of the existing 34 options.

By mid-1996 BA was looking at placing its first significant order since 1991, with the new additions likely to include Boeing 747-400s, 757s and 777s, the latter type probably being the first GE90-powered -300s.

In September 1996, the Korean operator, Asiana signed purchase agreements which included 10 Boeing 777-200IGWs and five 777-300s with options on a further five aircraft, all to be powered by PW4090/4098 engines. Deliveries were planned to start in 1998, with the 15 on firm order to be all in service by 2005. The order needed approval from the South Korean ministries of trade and finance, before confirmation.

Having been a loyal customer of Airbus over the years, as well as going through some serious economic problems, Air France received French Government approval to order up to 20 Boeing 777s towards the end of 1996, as part of its long-range fleet renewal programme. The order consisted of 10 777-200 IGWs, with 10 options to commence in 1998. The aircraft were to be powered by 92,000lb (409kN) thrust General Electric GE90 engines and will seat up to 288 passengers. The 777s would be complementary with the airline's A340s, and will be used on the high capacity North Atlantic route.

American Airlines signed an exclusive deal with Boeing in November 1996 worth $6.6 billion, to including at last firm orders for 12 777-200s and purchase rights for a further 38 aircraft to be confirmed between 1998 and 2018 for any variant. This was confirmed in June 1997, the 777s being the -200IGW version with deliveries commencing in 1998, but folding wingtips did not appear to be part of the specification.

Just over a week after the Boeing Board authorised the company to begin offering the new ultra-long range 777-200X

deliveries being two 777s in late 1998, two the following year, and three in 2000.

Towards the end of 1995 Delta was beginning to look for replacements for its ageing fleet of 56 TriStars, and was considering both the Airbus A330 and the Boeing 777. Following a comprehensive evaluation of all types of available aircraft, Delta concluded an exclusive 20-year fleet renewal agreement with Boeing in March 1997 for up to 644 aircraft, but at the time only 10 options were included for the 777-200s powered by Rolls-Royce Trent engines, the newly launched 767-400 being the replacement for the venerable TriStars.

Early in 1996 Malaysia Airlines (MAS) placed a combined order for Boeing 777-200s/300s, as well as for 747-400s, the 777 beating the Airbus A340 based on the higher seat capacity of the Boeing twin. MAS ordered a total of 15 Rolls-Royce

and the stretched -300X, MAS announced its intent by signing a memorandum of understanding (MoU) on 4 March 1997, to order 15 of the -200Xs in a deal valued at $2.1 billion. The MoU was signed during the roll-out ceremony of the airline's first of 10 777-200IGWs. Other carriers expressing interest in the -200X include Emirates, Korean and SIA. The design of the new version of the -200 was expected to be frozen in May 1998 with certification following in August 2000, allowing deliveries in September. The 200X is expected to be able to carry up to 298 passengers in a three-class layout over a range of 8,600nm (15,900km) allowing MAS to fly from Kuala Lumpur to Chicago, Los Angeles and New York non-stop. The timetable for the -300X is about four months behind the -200X.

BOEING 777 SALES

Airline	Version	Orders	Options	Engines	1st Delivery
United	-200	30	34	PW4073	15. 5.95
	-200IGW	4		PW4090	
ANA	-200	18	7	PW4084	31.10.95
	-300	10		PW4000	
Thai	-200	8		Trent	31. 3.96
	-300	6		Trent	
BA	-200	5		GE90	12.11.95
	-200IGW	10	15	GE90	7. 2.97
Lauda Air	-200	4		GE90	1997
JAL	-200	10	10	PW4000	15. 2.96
	-300	5		PW4090	
Emirates	-200	3		Trent	5. 6.96
	-200IGW	4	7	Trent	
Cathay	-200	4		Trent	9. 5.96
	-300	7	10	Trent	
ILFC	-200	6	2	GE90	
	-200/-300	18	2	10 GE90	
				5 PW4000	
				3 Trent	
China Southern	-200	6		GE90	
Air China	-200	5	5	PW4077	
JAS	-200	7		PW4084	3.12.96
Continental	-200IGW	5	5	GE90	9.98
Saudia	-200IGW	23		GE90	
KAL	-200IGW	4	4	PW4090	21.3.97
	-300	8		PW4090	
SIA	-200IGW	30	31	Trent	6.5.97
Singapore Air Leasing	-200IGW	6	10	Not specified	
Egyptair	-200IGW	3		PW	2.97
SAA	-200	4	3	Likely to be Trent	
Delta	-200	10		Trent	
MAS	-200	10	2	Trent	23.4.97
	-300	5	35	Trent	
	-200X	15		Unknown	
Asiana	-200IGW	10		PW4090	1998
	-300	5	5	PW4098	
Air France	-200IGW	10	10	GE90	1998
American	-200IGW	12	38	Unknown	
TOTALS		329	243		

ENTRY INTO SERVICE

With the major part of the flight development programme coming to an end, joint US and European certification achieved on 19 April 1995, and 180-minute ETOPS approval at the end of May, the Boeing 777 was ready to start earning its keep for the manufacturer and the airlines. The aircraft for United were overweight, but this was largely due to the furnishings, accessories, seating and fittings requested by the airline. The largest contributor to this weight increase was the new 16G crash-worthy passenger seats demanded by the latest certification standards, while Boeing was well within the contracted empty weight. The first visit to Heathrow by a Boeing 777 was when N7710A arrived during 18 April on a round-the-world flight, and the first aircraft was handed over to the airline at a ceremony at Seattle on 17 May 1995. The Boeing 777 entered service with United Airlines on 7 June 1995 when flight 921 operated Series 200A N777UA named *Working Together* departed London Heathrow for Washington Dulles International Airport. Other United 777 services started on the same day

BELOW: In December 1991 Emirates issued a letter of intent for seven 777s, with options on seven more. The initial order was intended for three of the early A-models, and four of the improved IGW versions. However, by the time the order was confirmed, it comprised four A-models and three IGWs powered by the Trent engines. Boeing 777-21H WA030 A6-EMD was the first for the airline, making its maiden flight on 2 May 1996; was delivered on 5 June 1996. Emirates was the lead customer for the Trent 890 engine, developing 90,000lb (400kN) of thrust, the highest in the world, for the IGW version, with deliveries commencing early 1997. *Boeing*

were linking Washington DC and Denver with Chicago, and the Frankfurt to Chicago services commenced the next day. As more aircraft were delivered, services expanded to include Paris to Chicago plus Newark and Amsterdam via London within a month. The United aircraft were configured with 292 seats in a three-class layout, with 12 First Class, 49 Connoisseur Class and 231 Economy. Every seat in the aircraft was fitted with its own phone and fax/modem point, a computer port and a sophisticated entertainment system. The entertainment system offers the capability of listening to the communications between the flight deck crew and the air traffic controllers.

Early service experience with the United 777s brought the expected minor problems, the most serious being a slow yawing motion which caused some air-sickness for passengers and cabin crew sitting in the rear of the aircraft. To cure this Boeing made some modifications to the gust response system. Another cabin comfort issue was snow inside the cabin when the moist air condensed, but this was cured by fitting ice screens in the outlets. Overall reliability was good, and in the first three months of revenue service with six aircraft the cumulative reliability was 97.7 percent, with a drop to 97.6 in the fourth month when turnaround times were reduced. By mid-1996 reliability was targeted at 98 percent, improving to 98.4 percent after three years of operation. The central maintenance computer was able to avoid delays caused by prolonged trouble-shooting or wrongly identified problems.

By early February 1996, United was becoming frustrated

with some of the niggling problems associated with the introduction of the 777s into the fleet, with 10 aircraft delivered.
Joseph O'Gorman, the United fleet operations executive VP
wrote to Ron Ostrowski, the Boeing 777 general manager on
13 February stating that the aircraft reliability and performance
was a 'major disappointment'. The text of his letter was as follows:

'United's 777 reliability and performance has been a major disappointment during the past few months. I am very concerned,
and would like to ensure that Boeing and United are taking any
and all actions necessary to fix these problems as soon as possible. The airplane Mechanical Schedule Reliability rate over the
past two months has been approximately what we expected. In
addition, the number of pilot write-ups and flight cancellations,
as well as the airplane out-of-service time, has been intolerable.

'There are a large number of issues that need to be addressed
in order for the airplane to perform at the level that Boeing and
United envisioned. Attached is the latest status of some of the
top issues which have the potential to cause the largest impact on
our 777 operations. Some appear to have good interim solutions
identified with aggressive timelines for final fixes, while others
look like they could be improved upon. The AOG (aircraft on
ground) team support is much appreciated and should be considered for every opportunity where it can be effectively employed.

'The large volume of work and lack of maintenance alloca-
tion, due in part to the strike, delayed the delivery schedule and
has significantly constricted our maintenance operation. We
need your ongoing commitment for extraordinary support from
Boeing in terms of more AOG teams to rapidly incorporate
solutions, more consignment spares for problem units, faster
turn times to incorporate unit modifications and faster timelines to reach design resolutions for major problems.'

This letter was obviously not intended for publication, but it
appeared in the *Wall Street Journal* on 6 March. It was simply a
typical communication between two professional engineers, and
United was quick to point out that the 777 was outperforming
all other new aircraft introduced into the fleet, the 777 being an
excellent aircraft which they wanted to make better. Boeing
claimed to be already aware of the problems listed, and the
AOG teams were working on the issues. By the end of
November, the despatch reliability had reached 97.5 percent,
which was well ahead of any other new aircraft, and the 777

BELOW: In the spring of 1993 Japan Air System (JAS) became the third major
Japanese airline to order the Boeing 777. In this case, due to a reduction of
passenger loads, JAS ordered seven A-model 777s in exchange for six 747-400s
previously contracted. The first 777-289 WA045 JA8977 for JAS made its maiden
flight on 23 October 1996 in a new livery specially designed for the new aircraft,
and was delivered on 3 December for services to start on domestic routes. *Boeing*

had reached a maturity stage in its introduction, when some problems would be expected to crop up.

Amongst the early problems encountered in service with the 777, and which attracted more than its reasonable share of publicity, was a precautionary diversion by a United 777 to Gander in July 1996 due to a loss of pressurisation. The failure, which was not a sudden depressurisation, was caused by a clamp cutting into the rubber boot ducting leading to one of the aircraft's two air-conditioning packs. The remaining pack could not maintain cabin pressure at the normal cruising altitude, so the crew reduced altitude to 22,000ft (6,710m) and made the diversion. The oxygen masks were not required, and therefore were not deployed. This incident followed two similar loss of pressurisation incidents in February 1995, which were also related to the failure of a clamp. These minor incidents were blown out of all proportion, and in relation to the overall reliability of a very complex and advanced aircraft, were the type of bedding in incidents which might be expected with any new airliner. Boeing were therefore achieving their goal of a service ready aircraft, if a few clamps were causing the only faults.

BELOW: At the end of 1992, China Southern placed the first order for Boeing 777s for the People's Republic of China. The first 777-21B made its maiden flight on 30 November 1995 and was delivered to the airline base at Guangzhou on 28 December 1995. The 777s are flown on high density regional routes. *Boeing*

United found that the introduction of the 777 on the North Atlantic routes, replacing the Boeing 767s, attracted new passengers to the airline, which soon achieved load factors of 86.9 percent by carrying more than 60,000 revenue passengers in the first month. With the delivery of the sixth 777 to United in November 1995, the airline commenced direct flights from Los Angeles to Washington DC. The 1996 programme took advantage of the increasing popularity of the 777 by scheduling two daily round trips between London and Washington DC, with a third departure to Dulles during the peak summer season using a 767-300ER. On 2 March 1996, United commenced 777 daily flights to Miami from Chicago, and then on to Sao Paulo in Brazil, as the first service with the 777 to South America, by which time the fleet had grown to nine aircraft. On 6 June 1996, the 777s replaced 767s on the Amsterdam to Chicago route, as well as increasing the flights from Germany with a new non-stop daily service linking Dusseldorf with Chicago. The 777-200As were used initially on transatlantic and US domestic feeder operations for transatlantic flights, and with the arrival of the 777-200IGW versions in the first half of 1997, they took over the transatlantic flights, leaving the earlier versions on the high density domestic US services.

After one year in operation with United, the 777 was claimed to have been an outstanding success, outperforming the rest of the airline's transatlantic fleet, by which time 12 777s

had been delivered. The noise levels of the 777 are 18 decibels below the current US and international standards, while nitrous oxide emissions are 44 percent below, making the aircraft a good neighbour at all the airports from where it operates. On 15 January 1997 United introduced the 777 on its London to Chicago service, replacing the 767s, by which time 16 777s had been delivered to the airline. With the delivery of the longer range 777-IGWs to United, a direct service from London to San Francisco was inaugurated on 31 March 1997, and was joined by a second aircraft on 11 April. As more of this version were delivered, non-stop daily flights also commenced between London and Los Angeles on 6 June.

The benefits of the 'Working Together' programme with Boeing, United and Pratt & Whitney are most apparent to the passengers. The 777 was the first aircraft to be market-driven, and built around the passenger needs. Throughout the development process, United review teams provided advice on a wide range of the aircraft systems, including engineers consulting on maintenance issues, pilots advising on flightdeck and avionics design, and flight attendants helping to improve galley design, and ways to improve overall passenger service. As a result the baseline design reflected the requirements of United, giving it the aircraft they wanted, not the one it had to settle for. More than 1,250 design issues were resolved, and amongst the key recommendations were the creation of ceiling stowage bins with easy access; easy to replace passenger reading lights; heavier gauge wire in unpressurised areas for improved reliability; improved wing access panels permitting easier access; reconfiguring the altitude selector on the flightdeck to select altitude changes faster and with greater accuracy; design of nose-wheel gear to accommodate a towbarless tractor; and the relocation of the refuelling panel, to allow the use of standard hydrant vehicles.

United's first 777 flew 1,000 flights before delivery, simulating the first two years of operation, validating long-term flight reliability, giving a full service ready aircraft on delivery for revenue service. Although Boeing flew many of these operations, 90 of the flights were under the total control of United pilots and maintenance crews, to satisfy an FAA requirement. One of the main goals of United was to provide passengers with the most comfortable aircraft ever developed, and this did not just include an extra 3in (7.5cm) on the width of the double seats, but aisles wide enough to allow passengers to pass the service carts, easy access overhead bins which pull down to 5.5ft (1.7m), but give overhead clearance of at least 6ft (1.8m) when closed. The Cabin Management System (CMS) enables flight attendants to manage cabin temperature, lighting and air conditioning throughout six different zones in the aircraft, giving faster response times, and a higher level of comfort and service level overall. United's Interactive Video System (IVS) offers the choice of six channels of video, 19 CD quality audio channels, plus video games and a full range of communications services at every seat. Located in each armrest is a lightweight handset, that serves as a phone, programme selector, game controller and credit card reader. In Economy Class individual screens are located in the seat backs, while in first class and Connoisseur, 5.7in (0.75cm) full-colour LCD video screens can be deployed from the armrest.

RIGHT: In early 1996 Malaysian Airlines (MAS) ordered a total of 15 777s. The first, WA064 9M-MRA, made its first flight on 26 March 1997. This Rolls-Royce Trent-powered aircraft was formally delivered to MAS on 23 April. *Boeing*

BELOW RIGHT: On 14 December 1993, Korean Air ordered eight Pratt & Whitney-powered 777-200IGWs, with options on a further eight stretched versions when they became available. The first 777-2B5, WA059 HL7350 for KAL, made its maiden flight on 4 March 1997 and was delivered to Seoul on 21 March for use on destinations in North America. *Boeing*

On 20 April 1995 N77779 flew into Heathrow for a brief public relations handover ceremony to British Airways, before departing the same night back to Boeing. Problems with the GE engines on flight test were threatening the official delivery date of 28 September, with planned service entry in October. An engine problem experienced during certification flight testing, was when compressor blade damage was caused on 18 August due to rubbing on the compressor case. The ETOPS certification of the GE90-powered 777s was scheduled for mid-December, with BA planning to make use of this capability early in 1996.

However, service entry was delayed due to some of the engine modifications requiring further testing, including a repeat of the icing tests on 1 October, which meant that there was no chance of meeting the original delivery schedule. Following successful tests at Edwards Air Force Base, which utilised a modified water-spraying KC-135 tanker aircraft, Boeing and GE faced the full FAA certification icing tests, which required flying around the USA looking for suitable conditions. Following FAA approval, the airframe/engine combination needed to obtain UK CAA approval, as well as the European JAA certification. Boeing were still hoping for an October delivery date for the first aircraft to BA, which the airline found acceptable, provided they had the first five aircraft by March 1996.

Continued problems with the GE90 engine development resulted in further delays, with certification anticipated by 7 November in the hope that the initial delivery could be made to BA by mid-month. By early November the second GE90 powered aircraft had completed about 240 hours out of the required 300 hours functionality and reliability (F&R) flying, with the test team looking for the correct weather conditions to evaluate the wing thermal anti-icing system. The engine finally achieved FAA type certification on 3 November 1995; this was followed rapidly with a recommendation for approval in Europe, and certification was finally awarded on 9 November, the UK CAA having satisfied their outstanding concerns. The first 777 was delivered to BA on 12 November, about two months later than expected, but with two more aircraft ready, it was anticipated that they would be delivered on schedule by the end of the year, with two more to follow by March 1996.

FIRST YEAR PROGRESS REPORT

One year after the 777 had first entered service with United, the progress to date was reviewed, by which time around 35 aircraft were in operation with eight operators around the world. Despite intensive efforts to identify as many potential snags before delivery as possible, it is only in intensive airline

service that some of them surface. The initial reliability of the 777 was outstanding, compared with any previous airliner, but unexpected snags were revealed during the first year, despite the intensive efforts to identify them before delivery.

A major part of the problem was the demanding set of performance targets set jointly by Boeing and the small group of launch airlines. The target of the service-ready aircraft with a despatch reliability of 98 percent on delivery was probably unrealistic, especially when airliners with less innovation take up to three years to reach these levels. Equally demanding was the aim to deliver the aircraft ready to be flown on ETOPS, which normally takes a number of years, and depends not only upon the manufacturers of the airframe and engines, but also the operational philosophy of the airline and local airworthiness authorities. While major experienced international trunk airlines like the majority of the launch operators of the 777, should have no difficulty complying, there are others who either do not have the background experience, or even the need for ETOPS.

In the case of the introduction of the 777 with United, despatch reliability was running at a high 97.9 percent one year after the type was introduced. The target was 98.5 percent, and it was showing signs of achieving these levels after 15 months. The overall world fleet was expected to achieve 98 percent reliability within 18 months of service introduction, which is not only high considering some airlines were only just receiving their aircraft, but it was well ahead of the simpler 767, and the more mature 747-400. With United, the 777 was worked hard from the start, averaging 10.5 hours per aircraft every day, and if the US domestic routes were ignored, the utilisation went up to 12 hours daily.

Examples of minor, but irritating, snags experienced during early operations was the icing of the No 4 passenger door arm/disarm mechanism, due to an undetected moisture path freezing around a cable seal. This door had not been used during the ETOPS trials, as the cabin was empty, but by rerigging and improving the sealing, the problem was solved. No amount of simulation could have reproduced this fault. Another problem was caused by a lack of service experience with handling cargo. Springs which activate the pop-up cargo container guides in the hold were breaking and had to be replaced with redesigned items. Another snag with springs was that the dual redundant ones which assisted the retraction of the main undercarriage, were cracking from the start of operations. It had to be demonstrated to the FAA that despatch could be made with only one spring, while replacement springs were designed. One of the three VHF antennas had to be removed from under the belly of the aircraft, due to electromagnetic interference from the electronics bay. The FAA insisted that all three VHF antennas be functional for despatch, which caused some unscheduled cancellations, and the affected antenna was repositioned to the upper aft fuselage. Electromagnetic interference is

RIGHT: British Airways placed its controversial order for the Boeing 777 powered by General Electric GE90 engines on 21 August 1991. The first aircraft for BA joined the test fleet as N77779 WA006 with a maiden flight of 5hr 20min on 2 February 1995. The Boeing 777-236 was later re-registered G-ZZZA and delivered to BA on 21 May 1996, the fourth out of the initial batch of five early aircraft to join the fleet. *Boeing*

very difficult to detect in advance, and was obviously not experienced during the flight development programme.

United started with a list of about 100 snags requiring Boeing attention, which was reduced to about 30 after the first year of operation, and all were being addressed. While there were a number of problems with the mechanical parts of the 777, the sophisticated electronic systems were working well, particularly the Aircraft Information Management System, which despite being expected to cause problems, was functioning well, thanks to the development work in Boeing systems test laboratory.

The engines were the cause of most of the early reliability problems during the first year of service, especially with the demands of ETOPS from day one. Of the three engine options, only the Pratt & Whitney PW4084-powered 777 was cleared for 180-minute ETOPS from initial service entry, and over 40 percent of revenue flights were operated under ETOPS conditions. There had been no in-flight shut-downs, and despatch reliability had been in the order of 99.9 percent, which was a strong selling point for Pratt & Whitney. However, this reliability was not achieved without a major effort on behalf of Pratt & Whitney, who stationed engineering teams at all major hubs, to address cracked oil-lines, slow engine starting and high oil consumption before they became major problems.

The performance of the GE engines was probably more critical: the problems encountered during flight-testing led to a failure to achieve instant ETOPS. BA was the introductory operator of this engine/airframe combination — the first time the airline had used a GE jet engine. A surge was experienced during a pre-delivery test flight, and two of the 777s had to be grounded at the end of January 1995, because of damaged seals in thrust reverser ducts. By careful monitoring of the seals, a higher level of reliability was achieved.

With ETOPS eventually approved for the 777/GE engine combination, BA commenced flights to Boston from London on 27 October 1996 .

At the end of the first 12 months, Rolls-Royce Trent engines were in service on seven 777s with three airlines, Cathay Pacific, Emirates and Thai Airways. Apart from some minor problems shortly after introduction by Thai in April 1996, which were soon rectified, the introduction of the Trent went very smoothly.

FLYING THE 777

Captain Kevin Mottram, Flight Manager, Technical, for the British Airways 777 fleet, is not untypical in his enthusiasm for the aircraft. Having been on the TriStar fleet with BA, he was conveniently available with the retirement of that type to work with the project group on the 777 engineering team from 1991. There were two groups in London and four more in Seattle, and Kevin was teamed with a group of London-based engineers, bringing flight operations and engineering together, something that — although obvious — had never happened before, but which was prompted by the Boeing 'Working Together' culture. The specification of the aircraft evolved over a period of three years, the duties of the teams being to check

available options, revue the Boeing designs and pass feedback to the Seattle-based groups, who then communicated with Boeing. BA learned a great deal from 'Working Together', which also included the airworthiness authorities.

From the outset ETOPS was a major issue, and worked closely with Boeing, GE and the CAA to determine what had to be achieved, what had to be tested and the presentation of the results. ETOPS was achieved 'out of the box' with the Pratt & Whitney-powered 777s, but the GE programme of 1,000 flights, of which BA would operate 100, was delayed by a number of engine problems. BA, therefore, started proving flights of its own, to learn about the aircraft before delivery. This was followed by 1,000 in-service cycles on the routes to Paris and the Middle East ahead of the Boeing test programme. In fact the first 777 to be delivered was flown daily between London, Muscat and Dubai during the first five weeks, and once four aircraft had been delivered, one was allocated to the intensive London–Paris route, while the others flew to the Middle East. The Paris run was useful for sector training for air and ground crew, and it provided a good back-up for the longer services, as a 767 could quickly be made available for the Paris route, and the 777 could be allocated to the Middle East run without any crew availability problems. The first 777 into service with BA, G-ZZZC experienced no technical problems for the first five weeks of operation — something unheard of with any previous new aircraft. It did, of course, benefit from a higher level of support than would be normal, but it helped the engineering team keep ahead of any potential problems, and learn about the aircraft.

By the time the BA flight operations team became involved in the definition of the aircraft, the basic architecture of the flightdeck had been established by the Boeing flight test pilots led by John Cashman. The BA team was able to influence the effect of flightdeck lighting, as well as the contents and symbols on the information displays. The crews made regular visits to the engineering procedures trainer, to allow observation of their actions and any mistakes as the design evolved.

The first 27 BA pilots, plus one CAA pilot, were trained in the Boeing training school in Seattle. Each course took a total time of seven weeks — three weeks in the ground school, three weeks on the full flight simulator, and the final week flying. The pilot flew to various destinations in the USA, acquainting themselves with the handling of the aircraft, take-offs and landings in a benign atmosphere, without the stress of normal route flying. The CAA pilot involved is the flight operations inspector, and continues to fly on the line at least once a month to maintain currency. These 27 initial pilots came from across the entire BA fleet, but those who had not flown ETOPS before

ABOVE RIGHT: The BA flight crews converted fairly easily to the new 777, having been given some prior experience of the twin-engine ETOPS operations on the 757/767 fleets. By the time BA flight operations were involved in the 777 programme, much of the flightdeck design had been completed, including retaining the conventional control columns. *Philip Birtles*

RIGHT: In the centre of the two-pilot flightdeck layout is the Engine Indication and Crew Alerting System display. *Philip Birtles*

spent six months on the 757/767 fleet to qualify, as well as in some cases gaining familiarity with the glass cockpit.

BA now has its own 777 flight simulator at Cranebank, supplied by CAE of Montreal, and may require a second one in the future. BA bought the Boeing-developed training course, which is computer-based, each candidate working through the course at his/her own rate on a PC. To become familiar with the new programme, the BA instructors evaluated the new PC-based 757/767 training programme, and the feedback from the pilots is that it is the best course they have completed. Following the ground school, a two-pilot crew have 10 four-hour sorties on the simulator before being allocated to line training in actual service. 95 percent of all actual flight training is done on line flying, with a very occasional need for base training on the aircraft. After 10 sectors it is normal for a captain to be cleared to be in command, and a first officer will be checked out. Although two pilots work through the training as a crew, once on line they split up, and no two inexperienced pilots are rostered together.

By the middle of 1997, 200 pilots had been trained to fly the fleet of 14 aircraft which would be in service during the year. Further crews will be trained in the latter part of the year, to cover the operation of four more 777s due for delivery in 1998. Eventually up to 300 pilots will be trained on the 777 fleet, the large number necessary because when the really long range flights are started, a third pilot will be carried to cover for crew duty hours. Apart from initial training, the flight simulator is also used for twice-yearly currency checks, which normally take two days, as well as to bring up to currency pilots who have not achieved a manual landing within the previous 28 days. In addition to the full flight simulator at Hatton Cross, there is also an engineering trainer which is used for procedures training. This is used for two hours a day during the three weeks of ground school training.

When flying the 777, pilots familiar with large jets feel completely at home. Although the aircraft is utterly conventional in its handling, the fly-by-wire control system has removed the unpleasant characteristics of flying a large aircraft. When the thrust levers are moved, there is no change in pitch, and when put into a banked turn there is no need for the conventional back-pressure on the control column, as there is no tendency for the nose to drop. Handling is very easy, and in

the unlikely event of an engine failure, Boeing has developed a rudder bias to avoid undue loads in maintaining a steady flight path. This rudder bias is new on Boeing airliners, but was a feature of the DH125 business jet developed in the early 1960s.

Although the 777 is fitted with a sophisticated flight management system, the pilots usually fly the aircraft from take-off to between 10,000 and 20,000ft (3,050–6,100m), before selecting the autopilot. Even working the automatic systems is a satisfying experience for the pilots, especially as there are so many functions which can be used and are learned over a period of time. The descent, approach and landing are normally flown manually, to maintain currency, but a number of Cat.3b autolands have to be made in a six-month period, to maintain full familiarity with the systems. The most challenging process for the new aircrew is to understanding the Flight Management System and the Autopilot Flight Director System. The controls are user friendly and the simplified flightdeck makes use of lessons learnt over earlier generations of glass cockpits, with the bare minimum of circuit breakers' and information available for the pilots to maintain a safe operation without unnecessary extra complication.

A demanding feature of the Boeing 777 is its ground manoeuvring. It has a larger turning circle than the 747, and the stretched 777-300 will be even worse. To alleviate this problem, Boeing is installing externally-mounted cameras, one under each side of the tailplane facing the main undercarriage in front, and another facing forward behind the nosewheel. The view will be accessed on one of the cockpit multi-function displays, and the need for these visual aids was highlighted by the airline pilots, when it was found that corners were inadvertently being cut off. It did not take Inspector Clousceau to follow the muddy wheel marks from the taxyway to the 777 stand at Paris.

ABOVE RIGHT: To make ground handling of the 777 easier, and to position the aircraft into the maintenance dock, BA use a low-profile power unit which pushes from behind the nose-leg. *Philip Birtles*

BELOW RIGHT: Once in the maintenance hanger, the large inboard main undercarriage door is lowered for improved access. The large six-wheel main undercarriage unit has a castoring rear pair of wheels to avoid tyre wear. *Philip Birtles*

BELOW: Ground manoeuvre camera flightdeck controls (see also p55). Camera views can be displayed on any of the shaded monitors. *Boeing*

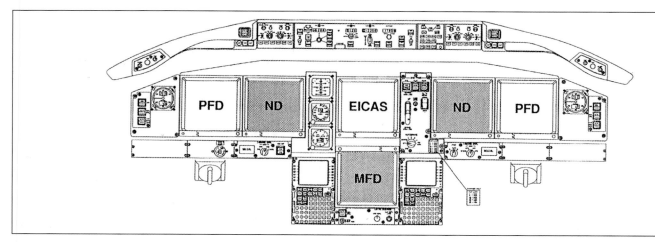

ALL NIPPON AIRWAYS

ANA took delivery of its first 777 in October 1995, the first in Asia, and services commenced in early December. The aircraft were used exclusively on domestic routes at the start. However plans are in hand to introduce the 777s on international Asian regional routes during 1997, as more aircraft join the fleet.

LEFT: A floodlit night-time shot of JA8197. *ANA*

RIGHT: The early 777s delivered to ANA featured the 777 logo on the fin. JA8198 WA021 made its maiden flight on 9 December 1995 and was the second to be delivered to Tokyo on 20 December 1995, where it was seen after push-back in June 1997. *Martin Prozesky*

BELOW: ANA took delivery of its first 777, JA8197 WA016, on 31 October 1995, the aircraft having made its first flight on 31 August. The aircraft entered service on Japanese domestic routes in early December. *ANA*

LEFT: ANA 777s JA8198 WA021 ready for departure and JA8967 WA037 just arrived at Tokyo show the two versions of the tail logo in use during domestic operations in June 1997. *Martin Prozesky*

BELOW LEFT: ANA 777 JA8967 WA037 first flew on 26 July 1996, and was the fourth to be delivered to the airline, on 12 August. Featuring the normal ANA logo on the fin, it is seen on arrival at Tokyo in June 1997. *Martin Prozesky*

RIGHT: An engineer with ANA contemplates the size of the Pratt & Whitney PW4084, one of three types of engine cleared to power the Boeing 777. *ANA*

BELOW: All Nippon Airways were included in the customer 'Working Together' teams, which helped to define the layout of the all-new 777 two-crew flightdeck. *ANA*

BRITISH AIRWAYS

Following delivery on 12 November, British Airways was able to commence services on 17 November from London to the Middle East destinations of Dubai and Muscat, increasing capacity by 15 percent when replacing the 767s on the route. As more of the 15 281-seat 777s on order were delivered, they replaced the 193-seat 767s on more Middle East routes, adding Abu Dhabi, Bahrain, Cairo, Jeddah and Riyadh to the 777 schedules. From April 1996 Kuwait was to be served daily, with flights to Amman increasing to four a week

When the 777 was introduced by BA, 15 flightdeck crews were trained. They had previously operated 757/767s, giving them experience in operating two-crew, glass-cockpit aircraft and ETOPS awareness. After the first year, 35 crews had been trained, coming from all over the BA fleet. The flight crews were pleased with the performance, reliability and handling of the new aircraft, the flight control system being particularly responsive, keeping good speed stability and trim. Ground handling is reasonable and the wheel brakes are very effective. The aircraft cruise speed was increased slightly from M0.83 to M0.84 as a result of operational experience, and the high temperature departure with full load from Middle East destinations is sufficient to reach the cruise altitude rapidly, avoiding low level ATC restrictions. PC techniques have been provided on the flight-deck with a 'mouse' being used to select items on the multi-function displays, electronic check-list, and the communications and reporting system.

The technical despatch reliability of the overall aircraft was about 96 percent after 12 months, with the engines achieving a creditable 99.9 percent. The engine fuel efficiency and environmental impact are outstanding, with approach and take-off noise levels less than the prop-jet British Aerospace ATP and United's Pratt & Whitney-powered 777s. The first five aircraft to be delivered were 777-200As, the last of this batch being used to test the slightly more powerful GE90-92B before it arrived with BA. The initial services with the 777s was from London to the Middle East and Paris, allowing experience to build up in operating the aircraft in short intense flights without the need for ETOPS. With the award of the ETOPS approval, transatlantic flights commenced, initially to Boston. The longer range 777-200IGWs, of which BA had 13 on order, allowed the introduction of US West Coast destinations.

For BA, 'Working Together' meant a better long-term fix

RIGHT: The flexibility of the 777 wing is quite pronounced when seen from close up along the leading edge. The early 777s were delivered to BA in the old livery, until the introduction of the new image in June 1997. *BA*

BELOW RIGHT: The second of the five initial 777-236s for BA was G-ZZZB WA010 which made its first flight as N77771 on 11 April 1995. After participating in the flight development programme to achieve certification of the 777/GE90 combination, the aircraft was delivered to the airline on 29 March 1997. It is seen here on approach to London Heathrow in May 1997. *Philip Birtles*

BELOW: British Airways introduced the new corporate image in mid-1997, the first 777-236ER G-RAES being delivered in the new colours in June ready for a brief appearance at the Paris Show before entering service. The aircraft was appropriately registered in recognition of the Royal Aeronautical Society. *BA*

for any problems, rather than having to be satisfied with an interim solution, while the manufacturer's design team developed a long-term answer. It was the first time all the skills had been brought together with Boeing, British Airways and GE all pooling their expertise. Apart from minor problems with the GE engines, Boeing delivered a service-ready aircraft, the first 777 entering service one week after delivery. The first 777-200IGW was in service two days after delivery, and the second was in operation the day after arrival at London Heathrow. Delays in entering service with previous aircraft have been avoided by fitting out the cabin fully with seats during manufacture, an innovation with the 777, which theoretically means that an aircraft delivered in the morning could be in service by the afternoon.

British Airways' prime concern in all its operations is safety above all else, and therefore when there have been any engine problems, the 777s have been withdrawn voluntarily from transatlantic flights until a suitable answer has been found. One example of an engine-related problem did not show itself until three months after the first aircraft entered service. It was found that the 'kiss' seals in the thrust reversers were splitting, and despite replacement continued to do so. The logical answer was to consider changing the seal material, until it was found that the cause was an unexpected resonant frequency in the associated ducting, which caused the metal to vibrate and damage the seal. The answer to the problem was to change the ducting design to remove the resonant frequency, which resulted in the aircraft being on the ground for two weeks. Once the aircraft returned to service, ETOPS operations were restarted, but were stopped for a short period when the bearings were found to be breaking up in an engine-related back-up generator, due to unexpected higher loads on the IGW aircraft. Although the aircraft were delivered to BA with full FAA and JAA ETOPS approval, the airline part of the operation had to be approved by the national authority, in this case the CAA. At least one 777 was used on a daily London to Paris flight, which not only helped to gain rapid experience of operating the aircraft, but also helped build up crew training experience. The remainder of the initial A-series aircraft flew to the Middle East, leaving the IGWs with additional fuel capacity in the centre tanks for the routes to North America.

BA now undertake all its heavy maintenance at Cardiff in Wales, using the Heathrow engineering facilities for the more transient maintenance. Currently the 777s are scheduled in on Thursdays and Fridays, when the S-check is carried out covering routine items, plus parts of a phased intercheck covering a two to two and a half year check on rotation, avoiding a long maintenance downtime. The S-check normally takes a team of about 20 people 24 hours to complete, and the comment is that the aircraft has been well thought out for maintenance. The biggest challenge for the engineering team has been the changing of an engine — mainly because of its enormous size. The first engine took three days to change but, with familiarity, this time has now been halved. All the supervisors and the management team, as well as training school instructors, were trained

by Boeing in Seattle, the course taking three months for 12 personnel at a time, followed by three weeks on the simulator to become familiar with the maintenance messages on the flight-deck, and the operation of the systems.

British Airways described the 777 as a robust aircraft, free from the traditional introductory problems and with mature systems from day one. Boeing's use of the SIL identified all the avionics problems before the aircraft entered service.

ABOVE: British Airways' new liveries may have come in for some criticism by ex-Prime Ministers, but there is no doubting the striking visual interest produced by the company's attempt to evoke the global nature of its operations with images from around the world. G-RAES features 'Delftblue Daybreak' — which combines traditional Delft colours of blue and white. The livery is designed by a one-time graffiti artist, Hugo Kaagman. *BA*

RIGHT: BA undertakes routine maintenance of the 777s at Heathrow, with all heavy maintenance at Cardiff in Wales. The aircraft is pushed into the specially constructed staging, giving access to all parts of the aircraft, and normally completes an S-check in about 24 hours. *Philip Birtles*

LEFT: Boeing 777-236ER G-VIIE made its first flight on 14 February 1997 and was delivered on 28 February. It is seen here ready for departure from London Heathrow in April 1997. *Philip Birtles*

BELOW LEFT: The first GE90-powered 777-236 for British Airways, WA006, made its maiden flight as N77779 on 2 February 1995, starting the development programme for the General Electric engine. It was delivered to BA on 21 May 1996, and is seen ready for departure from London Heathrow on 27 November 1996. *Philip Birtles*

BOTTOM LEFT: G-ZZZE was the last of the initial batch of five A-Model aircraft for BA. It was delivered on 13 December 1995, the third 777 to enter service. G-ZZZE is seen ready for departure from Heathrow in November 1996 followed closely by a sister ship. *Philip Birtles*

RIGHT: British Airways employees at Heathrow had their first view of a 777 on 20 April 1995, when WA006 stayed overnight for a public relations exercise. After being refurbished it was delivered to BA on 21 May 1996 as G-ZZZA. *BA*

BELOW: British Airways started to receive the 777-236ER — or IGW version — at the beginning of 1997. G-VIID was delivered on 19 February and is seen being pushed into the BA Heathrow engineering base for a regular B-check. *Philip Birtles*

CATHAY PACIFIC

Cathay Pacific took delivery of its first Trent-powered 777-200 in May 1996, as the lead aircraft in the orders for 11 777-200/300s with options on a further 10 to include future unspecified variants. The first 777 for Cathay was rolled off the Boeing production line in May 1995, making its maiden flight later in the same month, to start a development programme for the first Trent-powered aircraft. As part of the effort to achieve ETOPS before delivery, Cathay pilots and engineers operated the first Trent-powered 777 for 90 cycles, out of the total of 1,000 to simulate more than one year in airline use. These flights were made around the normal Asian and Australian routes in February 1996, giving the airline valuable operating experience prior to introduction. Following delivery to the airline, the initial 777 entered service with Cathay on 17 May flying from Hong Kong to Bangkok. A further three 777-200s were delivered between June and October, to bring the 1996 fleet total to four 777-200s, the remaining seven firm orders to be the stretched -300 version, with deliveries commencing in 1998.

The addition of the 777s to the Cathay fleet increased its flexibility, allowing the airline to match the varying levels of customer demand with an aircraft of appropriate size. The initial services for the 777s were the regional routes from Hong Kong to Tokyo, Bangkok, Seoul, Taipei and Osaka, and medium-range flights to Bahrain and Dubai. Later route developments are expected to add flights to the longer-range destinations of Sydney and Melbourne. The initial 777-200s were configured in a two-class layout, with 50 Business Class and 293 Economy Class seats. Advantage is also taken of the extra available underfloor cargo capacity. Although the design details are still to be finalised, the stretched 777-300s with Cathay are likely to seat up to 400 passengers in a two-class layout, which is almost the same capacity as the earlier 747s.

As their contribution to 'Working Together' Cathay provided input on operations, route structure, traffic loads, service frequencies and even local weather conditions. This resulted in a wide range of items, including satellite communications and global positioning systems (GPS) being specified as standard, instead of as more expensive options.

Cathay pilots who have converted to the 777 have commented on what a delight the aircraft is to fly, and how similar it is to the 747-400. The pilots started conversion training for the 777 at Seattle in August 1995, and around the same time the airline's full flight simulator was commissioned at Cathay Pacific's Hong Kong base. Initially the simulator was used for overall pilot training, apart from base training covering take-offs and landing, although once the aircraft were established in service, the simulator was used for the full flying training, up to the initial route flights and clearance.

RIGHT: Cathay Pacific 777-267 VR-HNB WA018 was the second aircraft powered by Rolls-Royce Trent 800 engines to join the flight development programme, and after refurbishment was the last in the initial batch of four A-market 777s to be delivered to the airline on 25 October 1996. The remainder are the stretched 777-367s for delivery in 1998. *Cathay*

After making its maiden flight on 4 April 1996, 777-267 VR-HNC was the first of four A-market aircraft to be delivered to Cathay Pacific in Hong Kong, on 9 May. It is seen here on typical night-time turnaround at Bahrain Airport.

LEFT: The scene outside Bahrain's terminal complex.

BELOW: There is sufficient clearance around the 777 for the two rear holds to be loaded and unloaded, while catering is supplied to the rear galley.

ABOVE RIGHT: Cathay 777 VR-HNC is finishing loading, ready for push-back and departure back to Hong Kong.

BELOW RIGHT: With the aircraft parked and the passenger finger dock in place, the forward cargo hold is loaded ready for departure.
All photos by PR Dept, CAA, State of Bahrain via Johann Prozesky

EGYPTAIR

Egyptair became a new operator of the 777 when the airline took delivery of its first 777-200IGW on 29 May 1997. The Pratt & Whitney-powered aircraft was the first of three for delivery to the airline during 1997, with two further aircraft on option, and is fitted with 319 seats in a traditional three-class layout. The 777s will be mainly operated between Egypt and the USA, with some flights between Cairo and Paris or London. The introduction of the 777 to Egyptair's fleet filled the size gap between the larger 747 and smaller 767, allowing the required levels of service in the most economic and efficient manner. Egyptair was awarded 180-minutes ETOPS from day one by the Egyptian Civil Aviation authorities, confirming the high operational standards and safety being achieved by the airline. The passenger reaction to the spacious and comfortable cabin of the aircraft was very favourable. As well as all the normal features available from the entertainment and communications system, passengers can watch the take-off and landing of the aircraft through a nose-mounted camera, as well as an air-show system which keeps passengers informed about the flight route, time, altitude, temperature and destination time.

BELOW: Egyptair took delivery of the first of three Pratt & Whitney-powered 777-266s, SU-GBP, on 29 May 1997 for operations from Cairo. *Egyptair*

BOTTOM: Soon after delivery of the 777-266IGW SU-GBP to Egyptair in May 1997, the three-class 319-seat aircraft was used on European destinations to gain operational experience by substituting it for other aircraft. It is seen here on approach to London Heathrow in mid-June 1997. *Philip Birtles*

RIGHT: Egyptair are fully qualified for ETOPS operations with the Pratt & Whitney PW4000-powered 777-266 aircraft. *Egyptair*

EMIRATES AIRLINES

The first of seven 777-200s for Emirates Airlines emerged from the production line in May 1996 to be prepared for delivery in June, followed by subsequent deliveries in July and October. The Dubai-based Emirates Airlines was formed in 1985, has doubled in size every three and a half years and has been profitable in all but its second year of operation. The government-owned airline benefits from a high proportion of its passengers wishing to use Premium Class service, which matches the phenomenal growth in the national economy of the United Arab Emirates. Yield, however, has been constrained by the competition from over 90 other airlines operating through Dubai, as well as absorbing the continual costs of the high growth. By organic growth Emirates plan to offer a more personal, high-quality service to their customers. Three of the initial seven Boeing 777s were in service by the end of 1996, with a further seven options due to join the fleet by 2000. Emirates make full use of the new cabin features, spending $2.5 million per aircraft on the in-flight entertainment system, including personal videos in every seat in all three classes. On board phone and fax services are also provided, which may not be always welcome, as a long intercontinental flight used to be a good way of getting away from the phones and leave time for constructive thinking. These new passenger entertainment systems are very advanced and have not been without introductory snags, but by having an engineer on board during the early days, most of the problems were solved on the spot. Emirates is responsible for the full maintenance of the fleet, which has allowed the airline to achieve a utilisation of over 15 hours per day. The initial three 777-200As are being followed by four 777-200IGWs during 1997 which will be used on services to Australia, South Africa and transatlantic operations, once the 777/Trent combination has achieved ETOPS approval. Emirates already operate 777s into London, through Heathrow and Gatwick, from where transatlantic

TOP: The second 777-21H to be delivered to Emirates was A6-EME WA033 on 3 July 1996, having made its maiden flight on 14 June. The first four of the initial order for seven aircraft were to the A-market standard and the final three were 777-21H ER versions similar to the -200IGW, the first of which was A6-EMH WA047 delivered in May 1997. A6-EME is seen ready for departure from London Heathrow in April 1997. *Philip Birtles*

ABOVE: The sophisticated in-flight entertainment system not only has a range of movies available, but also computer games for all ages, the screens being mounted in the seatbacks. *Emirates*

LEFT AND ABOVE LEFT: High above the clouds, Emirates first of seven 777-21Hs, A6-EMD WA030, made its maiden flight from Paine Field, Everett on 2 March 1996. *Emirates*

flights will be launched, as well as to Manchester. The seven aircraft on option will be 777-200IGWs with deliveries between May 1998 and mid-2000.

JAPAN AIRLINES

JAL accepted the first of 10 firm ordered 777-200s at a ceremony at Seattle on 15 February 1996, ready for services to commence on 26 April from the Tokyo domestic hub at Haneda to Kagoshima, later also serving Sapporo, Osaka, Nagasaki and Kumamoto. The aircraft were configured with 389 seats — 12 domestic First Class and 377 Economy. The five 777-300s on order will replace the ageing 747SRs on the denser domestic routes from 1998. Although the initial operations were on domestic routes, JAL is also considering eventually putting the 777s on international routes, but the timescale has not been specified. By the end of May 1997, JAL had taken delivery of five 777s, leaving five 777-200s to be delivered. Despatch reliability had achieved 99.5 percent with no unscheduled engine removals. Introductory problems were minor, and covered the same items as other airlines, examples including a VHF antenna problem and cargo-loading guide springs breaking. The JAL 777s are referred to as 'Star Jets' with each aircraft named after a major constellation.

For over two years, JAL was an active member of the 777 airline customer group in the 'Working Together' teams producing a much more versatile and economic aircraft. At the peak of 777 design, JAL had assigned more than 40 engineers to the 'Working Together' activities, some at the Tokyo-based engineering and flight operations departments, and others at Boeing at Seattle. In Japan, four groups worked on defining the flightdeck layout, maintenance manual definition, application of advanced technology systems and the 777 Stretch development. Cost-effective maintenance of the aircraft is critical to the airline, and much of the experience of the airline mechanics was incorporated in the design. JAL also made major contributions to the maintenance manual, which is written in English, and is a clear, practical and well-illustrated document.

JAPAN AIR SYSTEM

JAS took delivery of the first of its seven PW4084-powered Boeing 777-200s on 4 December 1996 for operation in a three-class layout on the Japanese domestic network. Although carrying full approval, ETOPS capability is not a requirement.

ABOVE: Japan Air System took delivery of 777-246 JA8977 WA045 on 4 December 1996, the aircraft having made its maiden flight on 23 October. *JAS*

TOP LEFT: The first 777-246 JA8981 WA023 for JAL made its maiden flight on 26 January 1996, and was delivered to the airline at Tokyo on 15 February named *Sirius*. The 389-seat aircraft commenced domestic operations on 26 April. *JAL*

ABOVE LEFT: JAL 777-246 JA8984 WA068 at Tokyo Haneda Airport. *Martin Prozesky*

RIGHT: JAS 777-246 JA8977, in a new livery specially designed for the aircraft, entered service on domestic routes in December 1996. *JAS*

MALAYSIA AIRLINES

In early 1996 MAS ordered a total of 15 777s, including five of the stretched -300, with options on two more 777s and a commitment to acquire 35 further aircraft as required. The first MAS 777 — designated -2H6 — was WA064 9M-MRA, and made its first flight on 26 March 1997. On the delivery flight this aircraft broke the great circle distance record when it flew non-stop from Seattle to Kuala Lumpur, a distance of 12,457 st miles (20,044km). The opportunity was then taken to continue around the world, back to Seattle, beating the eastward round-the-world record with an average speed of 553mph (889km/h), covering the 23,210 st miles (37,345km) in a time of 41hr 59min.

ABOVE: The Economy Class cabin of the Malaysia 777s has a 2-5-2 nine-seat abreast layout, with seatback screens for passengers to enjoy the entertainment and communications system. *MAS*

ABOVE LEFT: The Malaysia 777s feature a business centre for the First and Business Class passengers. It is equipped with a printer, fax, telephone, audio IFE, a multimedia library and reference materials. In addition every First Class and Golden Club Class seat is equipped with a PC point. *MAS*

LEFT: The Golden Club Class cabin in the Malaysia 777s is a 2-3-2 seven-abreast seat layout. *MAS*

ABOVE RIGHT: Malaysia Airlines took delivery of its first 777-2H6, 9M-MRA WA064 with 50th anniversary markings, on 23 April 1997. *MAS*

RIGHT: Entering a new dawn for the airline, the first 777-2H6 9M-MRA WA064 for Malaysia made its first flight on 26 March 1997, and was delivered the following month. *MAS*

SINGAPORE INTERNATIONAL AIRLINES

SIA took delivery of its first aircraft on 7 May, and introduced its first 777-200 into service on 15 May 1997 on its Jubilee B777 service to Jakarta, the first of 77 Rolls-Royce Trent-powered 777s which the airline has on order and option. The SIA 777s are deployed mainly on routes within Asia and Australia replacing some of the smaller capacity 189-seat Airbus A310s, and the destinations include Jakarta, Penang, Kuala Lumpur, Melbourne, Manila and New Delhi. Three more 777s were delivered in 1997, during the months of July, August and September, with in service dates scheduled for the first day of the following month. The aircraft are known as Jubilee B777s with SIA, as the first one was delivered as part of the airline's 50th anniversary celebrations. The SIA 777s are fitted with KrisWorld inflight entertainment and communications systems in all the 288 seats in the cabin, which gives the passengers a choice of 22 video channels, 12 audio channels, 10 Nintendo games, real-time text news and destination information on 16 cities in the SIA route network. In addition, there is an in-seat telephone allowing calls to virtually anywhere in the world. The aircraft cabin has accommodation for 12 First Class passengers, 42 Raffles Class with a 50in seat pitch, and the remaining 234 Economy Class seats in a 3-3-3 configuration.

ABOVE: Singapore Airlines first 777-212, 9V-SQA, was painted in special colours for the delivery on 6 May 1997, celebrating the airline's 50th anniversary. *Rolls-Royce*

BELOW: Using 777-212 9V-SQA, SIA commenced revenue services from Singapore to Jakarta on 15 May 1997. *SIA*

BELOW RIGHT: The Trent 800-powered 777 was introduced to service by Thai International Airways. Boeing 777-2D7 HS-TJB WA032 made its maiden flight on 30 May 1996, and was the second delivery to Thai on 13 June. *Rolls-Royce*

THAI AIRWAYS

The Rolls-Royce Trent 800-powered Boeing 777 was launched into service by Thai Airways, which took delivery of the first 777-200 of the 14 on firm order in April 1996. The initial services commenced from Bangkok to Hong Kong and Seoul. Flying in the Asian region, where growth levels are in excess of 10 percent, Thai Airways took advantage of over seven million tourists to the country in 1996, two thirds of whom came from the Asian region. Tourism generates over $4 billion in annual revenue for Thailand, often used as a stopping off point for travellers between Europe and Australia. Thailand also plays a major role in the wider Asia/Pacific economies, attracting a high level of business travellers. With the celebration of its 36th anniversary in 1996, Thai Airways had reached full maturity, with the best years to follow. With the introduction of the 777 into service in May 1996, the airline began the implementation of a new policy of reducing the number of aircraft types in its fleet from 13 to six by 1999. The 777 is playing a major role in the airline's development strategy, especially in the high capacity regional operations. Thai has an aim of being near the top of the world's top 10 airlines through improved efficiency, and because increased frequency is not possible to most of the destinations, the increased capacity of the 777 provides the answer to route development, without increasing congestion.

The initial eight 777-200s ordered by Thai are powered by the Trent 800 engine, rated at 75,000lb (333kN) thrust, which is 15,000lb (67kN) below the maximum certificated thrust because the aircraft is limited by its landing weight. The aircraft are configured in two classes, 55 seats in Business and 303 in Economy, with emphasis on the Business Class, which generates a higher revenue yield. By the beginning of 1997 the airline had four 777s in service, with one due in August, and the remainder to be delivered during 1998. Approval was awaited from the Thai government for the larger 777-300s powered by Trent 895 engines developing 81,000lb (360kN) thrust. This version would be configured with 455 seats, and the long-awaited government approval was delaying the overall fleet modernisation of the airline. By early 1997, the airline had 35 pilots trained on the 777, with a further six to eight in training at Seattle at any one time. Pilots with previous glass cockpit experience of the 747-400 spend 14 working days in the simulator, whereas other pilots need 23 days to familiarise themselves with the operation of the 777 systems. Pilots then fly the actual aircraft for two days, making between 16 and 22 landings, before going on to route training. Although the routes do not require ETOPS approval, Thai maintains the aircraft and crew training to ETOPS standards. The 777 has been found to be very similar to operate as the 747-400, with a well-balanced workload, and the only major difference being the attitude during the flare on the approach.

The 777s are used on the routes from Bangkok to Hong Kong, Seoul and Taipei, with an average utilisation of between 8.5 and 12 hours per day — not easy to achieve on the average 2.5-hour short sectors, together with the airport curfews. Plans were also being considered for the introduction of the aircraft on the Singapore and Osaka routes. Thai did not suffer from a high level of introductory problems, as the aircraft had already reached a maturity of service with other airlines. The introduction of the passenger entertainment system probably caused the most challenges, but the problems had been modest when compared with other airline experience. Thai is also responsible for the full maintenance of airframe and engines, as well as much of the equipment.

UNITED AIRLINES

United was the launch customer of the 777 and principal member of the 'Customer as Partner' group of airlines. The initial order for 34 Boeing 777s with options on 34 more was placed on 15 October 1990 as part of a mammoth $22 billion order, which included 60 747-400s. Engined by Pratt & Whitney, the United aircraft were scheduled for mid-1995 delivery: actual delivery of the first, the appropriately numbered N777UA, was on 15 May 1995 — a splendid production achievement. By spring 1997 United had received 33 of this order. The aircraft have proved user friendly for both airline and passengers, with high reliability figures: it is likely that they will continue in service for many years to come.

ABOVE LEFT: The first visit of a Boeing 777 to Britain was on 18 April 1995, when N771UA WA003 for United passed through London Heathrow on a round-the-world flight. This aircraft was delivered to United on 27 November 1995. *United*

LEFT: The first Boeing 777 to be delivered to United was N777UA WA007, handed over on 15 May 1995. It started the first commercial service from London to Washington DC on 7 June. *Philip Birtles*

TOP: With the commencement of delivery to United of the 777-222 IGW aircraft, the airline was able to start longer-range services from London, and gradually phase the initial shorter-range 777s on to the high density USA domestic routes. Boeing 777-222 IGW N785UA WA073 was delivered to United on 21 May 1997, and is seen on finals at London Heathrow on 10 June. *Philip Birtles*

ABOVE: After a year of operations, United was achieving a high 97.9 percent despatch reliability with the 777. N781UA WA040 made its first flight on 23 August 1996 and was delivered on 12 September. Just over two months after delivery, it is ready for departure from London Heathrow in late November. *Philip Birtles*

7 PRODUCTION LIST

c/n	Series	Airline Operator	Registration	Production Number	First Flight	Delivery Date	Remarks/Name
26916	222B	United	N777UA	WA007	25.4.95	15.5.95	
26917	222B	United	N766UA	WA008	4.5.95	24.5.95	
26918	222B	United	N767UA	WA009	17.5.95	31.5.95	
26919	222B	United	N768UA	WA011	31.5.95	24.6.95	
26921	222B	United	N769UA	WA012	13.6.95	28.6.95	
26924	222	United	N797UA				IGW
26925	222B	United	N770UA	WA013	26.6.95	12.7.95	
26926	222	United	N799UA				IGW
26927	222	United	N795UA				IGW
26928	222	United	N798UA				IGW
26929	222B	United	N773UA	WA004	28.10.94	31.1.96	
26930	222B	United	N772UA	WA005	19.11.94	29.9.95	
26931	222	United	N796UA				IGW
26932	222B	United	N771UA	WA003	2.8.94	27.11.95	
26933	222	United	N791UA				IGW
26934	222	United	N792UA				IGW
26935	222	United	N789UA				IGW
26936	222B	United	N774UA	WA002	15.7.94	29.3.96	
26937	222B	United	N776UA	WA027	3.96	11.4.96	
26938	222	United	N786UA	WA052	23.3.97	4.4.97	IGW
26939	222	United	N787UA	WA043			IGW

c/n	Series	Airline Operator	Registration	Production Number	First Flight	Delivery Date	Remarks/Name
6940	222B	United	N778UA	WA034	27.6.96	18.7.96	
6941	222B	United	N779UA	WA035	10.7.96	26.7.96	
6942	222	United	N788UA				IGW
6943	222	United	N790UA				IGW
6944	222B	United	N780UA	WA036	17.7.96	6.8.96	
6945	222B	United	N781UA	WA040	23.8.96	12.9.96	
6946	222	United	N793UA				IGW
6947	222B	United	N775UA	WA022	7.1.96	22.1.96	
6948	222	United	N782UA		14.2.97	7.3.97	IGW
6950	222	United	N783UA	WA060	24.2.97	11.3.97	IGW
6951	222	United	N784UA	WA069	16.4.97	29.4.97	IGW
6953	222	United	N794UA				IGW
6954	222	United	N785UA	WA073		21.5.97	IGW
7027	281	All Nippon	JA8197	WA016	31.8.95	31.10.95	
7028	281	All Nippon	JA8198	WA021	9.12.95	20.12.95	
7029	281	All Nippon	JA8199	WA029	2.5.96	23.5.96	
7030	281	All Nippon	JA8967	WA037	26.7.96	12.8.96	
7031	281	All Nippon	JA8968	WA038	2.8.96	14.8.96	
7032	281	All Nippon	JA8969	WA050	27.11.96	16.12.96	
7033	281	All Nippon	JA702A				
7034	281	All Nippon	JA703A				
7035	281	All Nippon	JA704A				
7938	281	All Nippon	JA701A				
7105	236	BA	G-ZZZA	WA006	2.2.95	21.5.96	
7106	236	BA	G-ZZZB	WA010	11.4.95	29.3.97	
7107	236	BA	G-ZZZC	WA015	1.9.95	12.11.95	
7108	236	BA	G-ZZZD	WA017	19.11.95	29.12.95	

BELOW: Emirates A6-EMD. *Philip Birtles*

c/n	Series	Airline Operator	Registration	Prduction Number	First Flight	Delivery Date	Remarks/ Name
27109	236	BA	G-ZZZE	WA019	3.12.95	13.1.96	
27116	200	Boeing	N7771	WA001	12. 6.94		Prototype
27247	21H	Emirates	A6-EMD	WA030	2.5.96	5.6.96	
27248	21H	Emirates	A6-EME	WA033	14.6.96	3.7.96	
27249	21H	Emirates	A6-EMF	WA042	25.9.96	17.10.96	
27250	21H	Emirates	A6-EMG	WA047	21.11.97	11.4.97	
27251	21HER	Emirates	A6-EMH	WA054		5.97	
27252	21HER	Emirates	A6-EMI	WA063	14.3.97	12.4.97	
27253	21HER	Emirates	A6-EMJ				
27263	267	Cathay	VR-HNC	WA028	4.4.96	9.5.96	
27264	267	Cathay	VR-HND	WA031	22.5.96	13.6.96	
27265	267	Cathay	VR-HNA	WA014	26.5.95	23.8.96	
27266	267	Cathay	VR-HNB	WA018	9.11.95	25.10.96	
	367	Cathay	VR-HNE			due 1998	
	367	Cathay	VR-HNF			due 1998	
	367	Cathay	VR-HNG			due 1998	
	367	Cathay	VR-HNH			due 1998	
	367	Cathay	VR-HNI			due 1998	
	367	Cathay	VR-HNJ			due 1998	
	367	Cathay	VR-HNK			due 1998	
27357	21B	China Sthn	B-2051	WA020	30.11.95	28.12.95	
27358	21B	China Sthn	B-2052	WA024	9.2.96	29.2.96	
27359	21B	China Sthn	B-2053	WA046	29.10.96	15.11.96	
27360	21B	China Sthn	B-2054	WA048	15.11.96	5.12.96	
27524	21B	China Sthn	B-2055	WA055	29.1.97	28.2.97	
27525	21B	China Sthn	B-2056	WA066	31.3.97	18.4.97	
27364	246	JAL	JA8981	WA023	26.1.96	15.2.96	*Sirius*
27365	246	JAL	JA8982	WA026	8.3.96	29.3.96	*Vega*
27366	246	JAL	JA8983	WA039	15.8.96	12.9.96	*Altair*
27483	236ER	BA	G-VIIA	WA041		7.10.96	1st BA IGW
27484	236ER	BA	G-VIIB			24.5.97	
27485	236ER	BA	G-VIIC	WA053	8.1.97	7.2.97	
27486	236ER	BA	G-VIID	WA056	3.2.97	19.2.97	
27487	236ER	BA	G-VIIE	WA058	14.2.97	28.2.97	
27488	236ER	BA	G-VIIF	WA061	3.3.97	20.3.97	
27489	236ER	BA	G-VIIG	WA065	31.3.97	10.4.97	
27490	236ER	BA	G-VIIH	WA070		8.5.97	
27491	236ER	BA	G-RAES			6.97	1st in new colours
27492	236ER	BA	G-VIIJ				
28840	236ER	BA	G-VIIK				
27493	236ER	BA	G-VIIL				
28841	236ER	BA	G-VIIM				
27604	2Q8	China Southern	lease from ILFC				
27605	2Q8	China Southern	lease from ILFC				
27606	2Q8	China Southern	lease from ILFC				
27636	289	JAS	JA8977	WA045	23.10.96	3.12.96	
27637	289	JAS	JA8978				
27638	289	JAS	JA8979				

c/n	Series	Airline Operator	Registration	Production Number	First Flight	Delivery Date	Remarks/ Name
	289	JAS					
	289	JAS					
	289	JAS					
	289	JAS					
27651	246	JAL	JA8984	WA068		20.4.97	21.4.97
27652	246	JAL	JA8985				
	246	JAL	JA8989				
	246	JAL	JA8990				
	246	JAL					
	246	JAL					
	246	JAL					
27726	2D7	Thai International	HS-TJA	WA025	1.3.96	31.3.96	
27727	2D7	Thai	HS-TJB	WA032	30.5.96	13.6.96	
27728	2D7	Thai	HS-TJC	WA044	7.10.96	25.10.96	
27729	2D7	Thai	HS-TJD	WA051	10.12.96	19.12.96	
	2D7	Thai	HS-THE				
	2D7	Thai	HS-THF				
	2D7	Thai	HS-THG				
	2D7	Thai	HS-TJH				
27945	2B5	Korean Air	HL7530	WA059	4.3.97	21.3.97	
27946	2B5	KAL	HL7531	WA062	14.3.97	28.3.97	
28408	2H6	Malaysia Airlines	9M-MRA	WA064	26.3.97	23.4.97	
28409	2H6	MAS	9M-MRB			5.97	
28410	2H6	MAS	9M-MRC				
28411	2H6	MAS	9M-MRD				
28412	2H6	MAS	9M-MRE				
28413	2H6	MAS	9M-MRF				
	2H6	MAS	9M-MRG				
	2H6	MAS	9M-MRH				
	2H6	MAS	9M-MRI				
	2H6	MAS	9M-MRJ				
	2H6	MAS	9M-MRK				
	2H6	MAS	9M-MSA				
	2H6	MAS	9M-MSB				
	2H6	MAS	9M-MSC				
	2H6	MAS	9M-MSD				
28423	266	Egyptair	SU-GBP			2.97	
28424	266	Egyptair	SU-GBR				
28425	266	Egyptair	SU-GBS				
28507	212	Singapore Airlines	9V-SQA		6.5.97		50th Anniversary
28508	212	SIA	9V-SQB				
28509	212	SIA	9V-SQC				
28510	212	SIA	9V-SQD				
28511	212	SIA	9V-SQE				
28512	212	SIA	9V-SQF				
	268	Saudi Arabian Airlines	HZ-AKA to HZ-AKW				
29111	45E	EVA Airways	B-16411			On order	

8 CHRONOLOGY

1986	Initial studies for an airliner with cabin size and range between the Boeing 747 and Boeing 767, using the 767 fuselage as a template.
1988	Group of eight prospective international customer airlines are formed by Boeing to advise them on the specification, operation and maintenance of the new airliner. In effect the start of the 'Customer as Partner' concept.
Oct 1988	When seven versions of the 767 did not provide the answer to the market needs, a totally new design was decided upon.
8 Dec 1989	Boeing Board approval for the marketing go-ahead of the 777.
Jan 1990	First meeting of the 'working together' airlines at Seattle.
15 Oct 1990	United Airlines places the launch order for 34 Boeing 777s, with options for a further 34 aircraft.
29 Oct 1990	Boeing formally launched the 777 programme.
Nov 1990	ANA order for 15 777s with options on ten more.
1991	Start of design.
21 Aug 1991	BA places order for 15 777s with options on a further 15, powered by GE90 engines.
Mid 1992	Production programme established, and stretched versions being studied.
Spring 1993	Major assembly of first aircraft established.
April 1993	First runs in the ground test cell of the GE90 engine.
8 Oct 1993	First runs in the ground test cell of the RR Trent 884 engine.
10 Nov 1993	First flight of P&W PW4084 engine in Boeing 747 testbed.
Nov 1993	Front fuselage of first 777 in final assembly.
6 Dec 1993	GE90 engine airborne for the first time in 747-100 test-bed.
Dec 1993	First 777 structurally complete.
9 April 1994	Roll out of first Boeing 777 at Everett.

ABOVE RIGHT: JAL 777-246 JA8984 is pushed back from its gate at Tokyo's Haneda Airport. *Martin Prozesky photo with permission of JAL*

BELOW: SIA 9V-SQA in the airline's special 50th anniversary colours. *SIA*

May 1994	FAA apprval of PW4084 engine.		at Paris Show with orders from ANA, Cathay Pacific, KAL and Thai.
12 June 1994	Maiden flight of first 777.	9 Nov 1995	GE90 777 combination certified.
15 July 1994	First 777 for United makes maiden flight.	12 Nov 1995	First GE90-powered 777 delivered to BA.
29 Dec 1994	ETOPS testing commenced.	17 Nov 1995	BA commenced scheduled services.
Jan 1995	Start of fatigue testing on complete airframe.	28 Feb 1996	RR Trent/777 ETOPS approval by FAA and JAA.
2 Feb 1995	Maiden flight of first GE90 powered 777 for BA.	April 1996	Thai Airways commenced commercial services with Trent-powered 777.
29 March 1995	First flight of RR Trent 890 engine in 747 flying test-bed.	Sept 1996	ETOPS approval by FAA of 777/GE90 engine combination.
19 April 1995	Certification of Boeing 777 by US and European airworthiness authorities.	Feb 1997	Boeing Board approved go-ahead of longer range 777-200X and 777-300X.
26 May 1995	Maiden flight of first RR Trent-powered 777.	March 1997	Assembly of 777-300 commenced.
30 May 1995	ETOPS approved by FAA for United/PW4084 engine combination.	Oct 1997	Maiden flight of 777-300.
7 June 1995	First revenue service by United Airlines.	Aug 2000	Hoped for certification date of 777-200X.
June 1995	Boeing announced launch of stretched 777-300	Jan 2001	Expected service entry of 777-300X.

INDEX